TUTOR ASSESSMENT PACK

MATHS

— YEAR 6 —

MATHS
— YEAR 6 —

CONTENTS

CONTENTS

How to use this pack

This *Tutors' Guild* Year 6 Maths Tutor Assessment Pack is full of assessment opportunities to help you prepare your student for the Key Stage 2 national curriculum tests. You can keep a record of your student's achievements using the progress tracker on pages 9–10. Everything in this pack is available for you to download as an editable file. This means that every test can be edited to suit the needs of an individual student, but also that you can print off each resource as many times as you need.

Types of test

The pack comprises three types of test, detailed below.

Checkpoint challenges

These tests are designed to each assess one subject area from the Maths curriculum: algebra; number, ratio and algebra and geometry, measurement and statistics. The algebra test should take around 30 minutes to complete while the others will take around an hour, but the challenges don't need to be strictly timed.

Each challenge will cover content taught during the corresponding lessons in the *Tutors' Guild* Year 6 Maths Tutor Delivery Pack (ISBN 978 1 292 17253 8). Checkpoint challenges – with the exception of the arithmetic challenge – are not designed to be exam-style but the content they cover is taken from the content domain of the mathematics test framework (see pages 7–10 of the Tutor Delivery Pack for more on the mathematics curriculum). Because Paper 1: arithmetic is potentially intimidating in layout, students are given extra practice in working in boxes in the arithmetic challenge. The geometry, measurement and statistics challenge and the number, ratio and algebra challenge replicate the style of the Tutor Delivery Pack activity sheets: familiar, unintimidating and engaging.

Checkpoint challenges can be used at any time during the course of tutoring – as a diagnostic at the beginning of the year or as revision before the tests, for example – but the most useful time to use them is at the end of each subject area as a summative test of your student's knowledge. The challenge may reveal an area in which your student lacks confidence and assessment throughout the year gives you plenty of time to address those areas.

There is a set of answers for every checkpoint challenge, with guidance on mark allocation where appropriate, at the back of this pack.

Topic tests

For every lesson in the Tutor Delivery Pack, there is a topic test. These shorter tests each have ten marks and should take around 20 minutes to complete. They have the same friendly, accessible look as the Tutor Delivery Pack activity sheets, to make assessment much less stressful for your student while allowing you to regularly and effectively track progress.

As with every aspect of the *Tutors' Guild* series, topic tests are designed to be completely flexible. Tutors with more than an hour per lesson may choose to complete the test at the end of the lesson or at the beginning of the next, to test knowledge retention. Equally, the tests are short enough that they can be given to students to complete during the week, instead of or alongside the suggested homework activity for the lesson. You may also wish to use the topic tests to revisit topics with which your student struggled when completing the checkpoint challenges or practice paper.

Answers to all tests are provided at the back of this pack.

Practice papers

In order to successfully prepare your student for the Key Stage 2 national curriculum tests, you should ensure they have the chance to experience 'exam-style' assessment. The practice papers in this pack give your student the perfect opportunity to become accustomed to the layout and demands of the national curriculum tests. For more on the content and style of the tests, see pages 7–8.

To get the most out of the practice papers, you may wish to have your student complete them well in advance of the test. This will ensure you have time to address any difficulties that become apparent. As there are three papers, it is advisable to complete them over a period of several weeks, so as not to put your student under too much pressure.

Answers and mark schemes are provided at the back of this pack.

HOW TO USE THIS PACK

PROGRESS TRACKING

On pages 9–10 of this pack, you will find a progress tracker to fill in every time your student completes an assessment. There is space on the tracker for you to record a first and second attempt at each test, if you wish to do so. When your student completes a test, look closely at the results and try to pick out patterns in their mistakes. Make a note of these patterns in the 'areas to work on' column so that you can use your future contact time together most effectively. You may wish to fill in the page called 'talk about the test' (page 11–12) with your student to find out which questions they found the hardest to answer, particularly if the test doesn't reveal much because your student didn't get many questions wrong.

INFORMATION FOR PARENTS

The information for parents provided on pages 5–6 of this pack is very similar to that in the Tutor Delivery Pack. This has been repeated for tutors who have decided to purchase one of the packs but not the other. If the parents of your student have seen the information in the Tutor Delivery Pack, you may just wish to explain the different types of test to them.

CERTIFICATES

In the digital version of this pack, you will find two customisable certificates. These can be edited to celebrate achievements throughout the year.

WORKING OUT SHEET

Included in the digital version of this pack is a page of working out boxes designed to replicate those used in the arithmetic exam. You can use these in two ways: to create your own arithmetic test and to provide extra working out space, particularly when place value is important.

INFORMATION FOR PARENTS

INTRODUCTION

Your child's tutor will often make use of resources from the *Tutors' Guild* Year 6 maths series. These resources fit perfectly with the current national curriculum tests. The tutor will use their expert knowledge and judgement to assess your child's current needs. This will allow them to target areas for improvement, build confidence levels and develop skills as quickly as possible, giving your child the chance to succeed in the end of Key Stage 2 tests or in their Year 7 resits.

Just as a classroom teacher might do, your tutor will use practice papers and tests to prepare your child for the new national curriculum tests, formerly known as SATs. Each set of resources has been designed by experts in primary maths and reviewed by experienced classroom teachers and tutors to ensure it offers great quality, effective and enjoyable assessment. All *Tutors' Guild* resources are fully flexible and adaptable so that your tutor can tailor the course to meet your child's needs.

TYPES OF TEST

Checkpoint challenge

Checkpoint challenges are designed to test your child's knowledge of a whole area of maths. There are three challenges: one in arithmetic; one in number, ratio and algebra and one in geometry, measurement and statistics. Because there is a whole test on arithmetic and because that test can appear quite intimidating to children, the arithmetic challenge looks just like the end of Key Stage 2 test. This gives your child time to get used to the format. The other two checkpoint challenges are more child-friendly in design, while still testing the topics your child will come across in the national curriculum test.

Your tutor may decide to complete the challenges during teaching time. This may depend on your child's confidence levels or reading ability, or it may be that they want to assess your child more informally and to discuss the challenge while completing it. Otherwise, your tutor will give your child the challenge to complete for homework. The arithmetic challenge will take around 30 minutes to complete, whereas the other tests will take around an hour. If your child is completing the challenge for homework, you don't need to time them strictly.

Topic tests

Topic tests are short, 20-minute tests that are worth ten marks each. They are designed to be fun and unintimidating for your child. They test much smaller areas – or topics – of maths. Whereas there is a checkpoint challenge testing all arithmetic skills, there are individual topic tests for each of addition, subtraction, multiplication and division, amongst others. There are 38 topic tests in total, which is enough for one per school week. Again, if your child completes a test for homework, you do not need to time their completion.

Practice papers

The *practice papers* replicate the tests that your child will sit at the end of Year 6. See page 6 for a breakdown of these tests. If your child is given a practice paper you may want to provide a quiet environment and time it more strictly so their experience of the paper is closer to 'the real thing'.

FURTHER SUPPORT FOR YOUR CHILD

Parents often ask a tutor what else they can do to support their child's learning or what resources they can buy to provide extra revision and practice. As a Pearson resource, *Tutors' Guild* has been designed to complement the popular *Revise* series. Useful titles you may wish to purchase include:

- *Revise* KS2 SATs Mathematics Revision Guide – Expected Standard (ISBN 978 1 292 14626 3)
- *Revise* KS2 SATs Mathematics Revision Workbook – Expected Standard (ISBN 978 1 292 14628 7)
- *Revise* KS2 SATs Mathematics Practice Papers (ISBN 978 1 292 14624 9)
- *Revise* KS2 SATs Mathematics – Geometry, Measure, Statistics – Targeted Practice (ISBN 978 1 292 14622 5)
- *Revise* KS2 SATs Mathematics – Arithmetic – Targeted Practice (ISBN 978 1 292 14621 8)
- *Revise* KS2 SATs Mathematics – Number, Ratio, Algebra – Targeted Practice (ISBN 978 1 292 14623 2)

'Above expected standard' editions of the Revision Guide and Revision Workbook are available.

MATHS
— YEAR 6 —

INFORMATION FOR PARENTS

WHAT'S IN THE TEST?

You may have heard a lot about the new national curriculum tests from your child's school, from other parents or in the media. Below is a breakdown of the tests that your child will sit at the end of Year 6.

ARITHMETIC

Your child will sit one test that assesses their arithmetic ability – their ability to add, subtract, multiply and divide whole numbers, fractions, decimals and percentages.

Paper 1: Arithmetic

This is a 30-minute test in which your child will be given a series of arithmetic questions worth 40 marks in total. The questions will not be contextual (there won't be any characters, items or measurements, just calculations to do) and will mostly be worth one mark each. Long division and multiplication questions will be worth two marks each. For two-mark questions, your child can get one mark for using an appropriate method, even if the final answer isn't correct. Every answer will be numerical.

MATHEMATICAL REASONING

Your child will sit two tests to assess their problem-solving and reasoning skills. There are no differences in the length, marks or types of questions in the two papers.

Papers 2 and 3: Mathematical reasoning

These tests are 40 minutes each and will be held on different days during the testing period. Each paper is worth 35 marks and uses a mixture of verbal (numbers and words) and non-verbal (matching, drawing lines/arrows) responses to test your child's ability to solve mathematical problems. Some of the questions will be contextual, which means that they will be set in real-world scenarios that your child should be familiar with, such as buying something in a shop or reading a bus timetable.

RESULTS

On results day, your child will not receive a grade or level as students do for their GCSEs or A levels. Instead, they will be given a scaled score for each subject. It is scaled so that there is no difference from year to year. If your child's score is 100 or higher, they are thought to be working at the expected standard for their age. If their score is 99 or lower, they are thought to be working below the expected standard.

ASSESSMENT GUIDANCE

At the end of Year 6, your student will sit three papers as part of the Key Stage 2 maths national curriculum tests. Below you will find a summary of what to expect. You can find full details about all of the papers in the mathematics framework on the government's website.

ARITHMETIC

Paper 1: arithmetic

Students will have 30 minutes to complete all of the questions on the paper (generally there are 36 questions). The paper is worth 40 marks, with the majority of questions worth one mark each. The only questions worth two marks are long multiplication and long division. There will be no context to any of the questions – they are just straightforward calculations – and every question will be laid out the same (see the *practice paper*, pages 87–99).

MATHEMATICAL REASONING

Papers 2 and 3: reasoning

Papers 2 and 3 are identical in timing, mark allocation and format. Each paper is 40 minutes, worth 35 marks and comprises a combination of contextual and non-contextual questions. Contextual questions involve a scenario, such as: *This table shows the temperature in six cities on the same day in January. Which city was the coldest on that day?* There are working out marks available for questions laid out in a box similar to those in Paper 1.

COGNITIVE DOMAIN

In the accompanying Tutor Delivery Pack to this title, the content domain for the Year 6 tests is explained. The content domain details the topics that may be covered in the test, whereas the cognitive domain explains the skills and processes required to respond to a question.

The cognitive domain is separated into four 'strands'. Each question in the test sits somewhere on a scale from 1 (low) to 4 (high) in each strand. The distribution of marks per strand is given in brackets. As you'll see, the majority of questions are in the lower to middle range band.

Depth of understanding (level 1: 30–70%; level 2–3: 30–70%; level 4: 10–20%)
Depth of understanding looks at what a student has to do to arrive at an answer.

- A level 1 or 2 question requires either recall of a mathematical fact or method, or the ability to use it to solve a simple problem, such as an arithmetic question.
- To find the answer to a level 3 question, the student needs to use the fact or method to solve a more complex problem.
- Level 4 questions require the application of the fact or method to a problem in a more creative way. This may be quite complex or unfamiliar in format, such as explaining how a number fact can be used to work out the answer to a different yet related calculation.

Computational complexity (level 1: 0–30%; level 2–3: 60–100%; level 4: 10–20%)
Computational complexity looks at how many steps there are to solving a problem.

- A level 1 question requires no numeric steps. There are very few questions of this kind, but an example could be a question asking the student to name a shape.
- Level 2 questions require one or a small number of simple numeric steps.
- Level 3 questions require a larger number of simple steps, such as adding up how much money someone has spent and taking that amount away from the total to find the amount they have left.
- A level 4 question will similarly require a larger number of steps but at least one step will be complex, such as carrying digits in a long multiplication.

ASSESSMENT GUIDANCE

Spatial reasoning and data interpretation (level 1: 60–80%; level 2–3: 0–20%; level 4: 0–10%)
There are two strands to this domain: spatial reasoning means understanding and working with geometrical problems; data interpretation is the understanding and interpretation of information in statistical form – that is tables, pictograms, charts and graphs.

- Level 1 questions present all of the information needed for the student to arrive at a correct answer. Such a question could ask the student to find the perimeter of a shape with all measurements provided.
- A level 2 or 3 question requires the student to work with the information given in the question. This might mean reflecting or translating a shape, interpreting a graph to find the most popular pet in a class or working out how many respondents chose red as their favourite colour from the size of a pie chart 'slice'.
- At level 4, students will be required to use inference to arrive at an answer or to generate new information from what is provided in the question. This could include the requirement for a student to identify 3D characteristics from a 2D representation of a shape, or to infer new information from given data.

Response strategy (level 1: 40–70%; level 2–3: 40–70%; level 4: 0–10%)
This strand measures the level of response required from the student.

- Level 1 questions may require the student to fill in a box or select a correct answer from several options.
- Level 2 questions require the student to follow clearly set-out steps to arrive at an answer. The student may be required to show their working.
- At level 3, the student will need to put together a straightforward response. They may also need to give a simple, written explanation for their answer.
- At the highest level of this strand, the student is expected to organise a complex response. For example, a multi-step question that requires the use of at least one method would expect the student to decide which calculations to use, to know the order in which to use them and to select the important information to carry through to the next step.

You should use the information above to inform your assessment of Key Stage 2 maths. If you create your own resources to accompany the *Tutors' Guild* series, it is useful to consider the distribution of marks per cognitive domain so that you are stretching students at a level similar to that of the national curriculum tests.

RESULTS

Previously, when students received their results from the Year 6 SATs papers, they were given a level between 2 and 6. This is no longer the case, as students are now given a scaled score for each subject: maths; reading; writing and grammar, punctuation and spelling. If the score is 100 or higher, the student is deemed to be working at the 'expected standard'. The score is scaled so that there is no differentiation in results from year to year, regardless of the perceived difficulty of any paper.

PROGRESS TRACKING

The progress tracker below will help you to record and recall your student's scores and performances as you work through this pack. As you may wish to use a test more than once (at the start and end of teaching a subject area, for example), there is space for you to record two scores for each test. There is also space for you to make notes on areas for further study.

	FIRST TRY	SECOND TRY	AREAS TO WORK ON
CHECKPOINT CHALLENGES			
Arithmetic	/40	/40	
Number, ratio and algebra	/40	/40	
Geometry, measurement and statistics	/40	/40	
TOPIC TESTS			
1 Diagnostic lesson	/10	/10	
2 Place value	/10	/10	
3 Rounding	/10	/10	
4 Estimating	/10	/10	
5 Addition	/10	/10	
6 Subtraction	/10	/10	
7 Multiples and factors	/10	/10	
8 Squares and cubes	/10	/10	
9 Multiplication	/10	/10	
10 Division	/10	/10	
11 Order of operations	/10	/10	
12 Proper fractions	/10	/10	
13 Fractions greater than 1	/10	/10	
14 Adding and subtracting fractions	/10	/10	
15 Multiplying fractions and decimals	/10	/10	
16 Dividing fractions and decimals	/10	/10	
17 Percentages	/10	/10	
18 Equivalence	/10	/10	

PROGRESS TRACKING

	FIRST TRY	SECOND TRY	AREAS TO WORK ON
19 Ratio	/10	/10	
20 Scale factors	/10	/10	
21 Simple formulae	/10	/10	
22 Linear sequences	/10	/10	
23 Two unknowns	/10	/10	
24 Scales and units	/10	/10	
25 Working with units	/10	/10	
26 Time	/10	/10	
27 Perimeter	/10	/10	
28 Area of a rectangle	/10	/10	
29 Areas of other shapes	/10	/10	
30 Volume	/10	/10	
31 2D shapes	/10	/10	
32 3D shapes	/10	/10	
33 Angles	/10	/10	
34 Transformations	/10	/10	
35 Tables	/10	/10	
36 Charts	/10	/10	
37 Line graphs	/10	/10	
38 Mean averages	/10	/10	
PRACTICE PAPERS			
Paper 1: arithmetic	/40	/40	
Paper 2: reasoning	/35	/35	
Paper 3: reasoning	/35	/35	

MATHS
— YEAR 6 —

TALK ABOUT THE TEST

Look at the test you have recently taken. Fill in the boxes with help from your tutor.

The test I took was …
(Your tutor will fill this in.)

My score was …

/

I felt …
(Circle the face that best describes how you felt when you took the test.)

😊 confident about the test.

😐 unsure about the test.

☹️ really confused about the test.

Next time I do a test, I will …
(What could you do differently? Did you rush through? Did you read the questions properly?)

The questions I found easiest were …
(Which questions did you find easy?)

because …
(Explain why you found these questions easy. Maybe you find tick box questions easy or prefer to explain your answer. Perhaps you have practised the topic a lot at school.)

TALK ABOUT THE TEST

The questions I found hardest were …
(Which questions did you find tricky?)

because …
(Explain why you found these questions tricky.)

To improve these areas, we are going to …
(Here your tutor will explain how he/she is going to help you become confident in these areas.)

At home, we can …
(Here your tutor will explain what you can do at home to become more confident in these areas.)

CHECKPOINT CHALLENGES

HOW TO USE

Each of these checkpoint challenges is intended to cover one of the main topic areas addressed in the national curriculum tests: arithmetic; number, ratio and algebra; and geometry, measurement and statistics.

Each challenge can be used in a number of ways:

- as a diagnostic test
- as a homework activity
- as a main activity if extra time is available
- as revision closer to the tests
- at the end of the relevant section of the lesson plans.

These challenges are designed to provide informal test practice, in addition to the more formal practice papers on pages 87–123.

ARITHMETIC CHALLENGE

The arithmetic checkpoint challenge has 40 marks in total, and should take around 30 minutes to complete.

It is designed to test the same skills as Paper 1 of the Key Stage 2 test. The questions are context-free and will test arithmetic skills.

For questions that say *show your method*, it is particularly important that the student shows their working out in the grids provided.

Answers can be found on page 124.

NUMBER, RATIO AND ALGEBRA CHALLENGE

The number, ratio and algebra challenge has 40 marks in total, and should take around an hour to complete.

It is designed to be similar in style to Papers 2 and 3 of the Key Stage 2 test. There are a mixture of contextual and context-free questions.

Where an answer box is provided, the student should show their working out. If an answer line is provided, the student only needs to write their answer.

Answers can be found on page 125.

GEOMETRY, MEASUREMENT AND STATISTICS CHALLENGE

The geometry, measurement and statistics challenge has 40 marks in total, and should take around an hour to complete.

It is designed to be similar in style to Papers 2 and 3 of the Key Stage 2 test. There is a mixture of contextual and context-free questions.

Where an answer box is provided, the student should show their working out. If an answer line is provided, the student only needs to write their answer.

Answers can be found on pages 126–127.

ARITHMETIC CHALLENGE

Do your working out on the grid and write your answer in the white box.

WORKED EXAMPLES

811 + 342 =

	8	1	1
	3	4	2
1	1	5	3

1,153

1 mark

Show your method

	4	3	2
x		2	3
8	6	4	0
1	2	9	6
9	9	3	6
	1		

9,936

2 marks

ARITHMETIC CHALLENGE

1   907 + 100 =

1 mark

2   51 + 257 =

1 mark

3   435 ÷ 10 =

1 mark

ARITHMETIC CHALLENGE

4

576 − 9 =

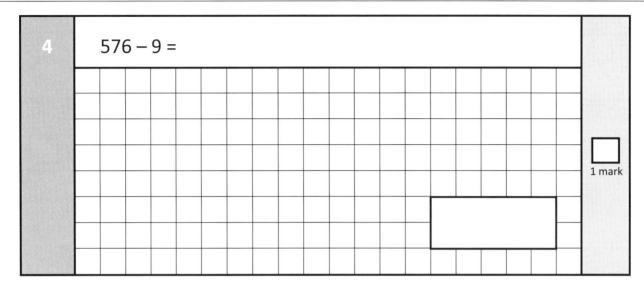

1 mark

5

876 + 246 =

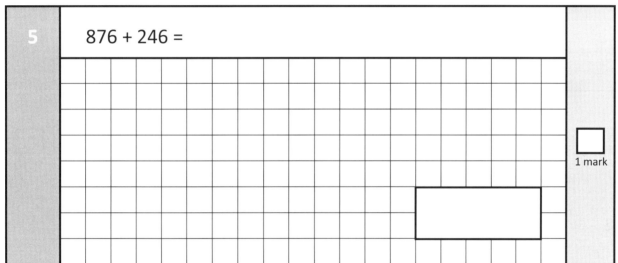

1 mark

6

96 ÷ 6 =

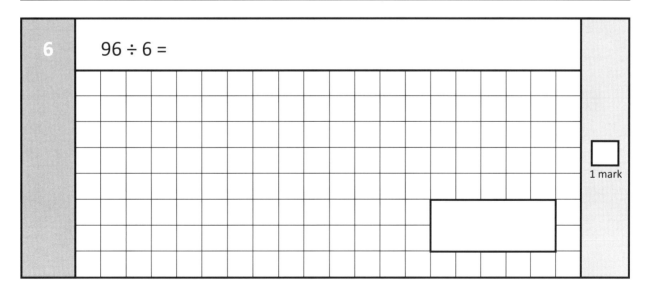

1 mark

ARITHMETIC CHALLENGE

7   35,967 + 6,548 =

1 mark

8   785 − 80 =

1 mark

9   480 ÷ 8 =

1 mark

ARITHMETIC CHALLENGE

10   643 × 3 =

1 mark

11   9 × 7 =

1 mark

12   70 × 80 =

1 mark

ARITHMETIC CHALLENGE

13

$1{,}000 \times 318 =$

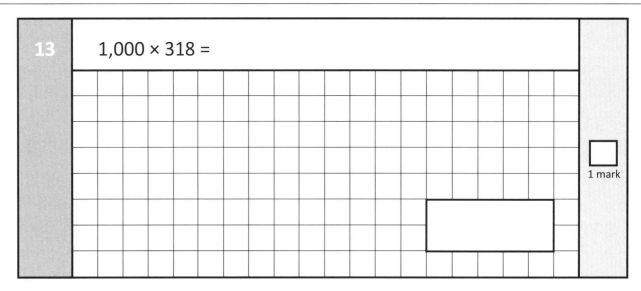

1 mark

14

$7{,}007 + 238 =$

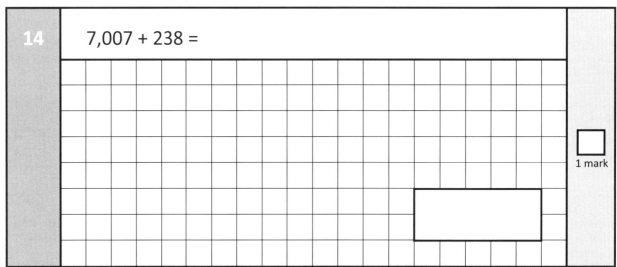

1 mark

15

$378 \div 3 =$

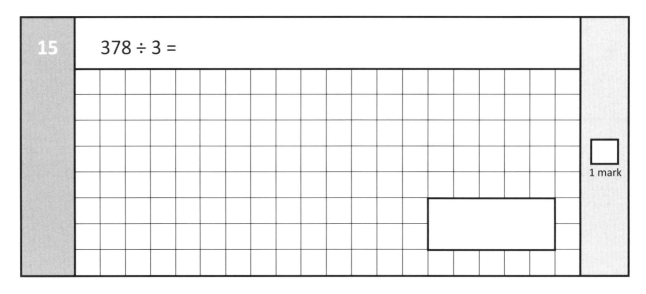

1 mark

ARITHMETIC CHALLENGE

16   19.45 + 28.737 =

1 mark

17   234.59 − 156.4 =

1 mark

18   138,765 − 9,999 =

1 mark

ARITHMETIC CHALLENGE

19 $4^2 + 100 =$

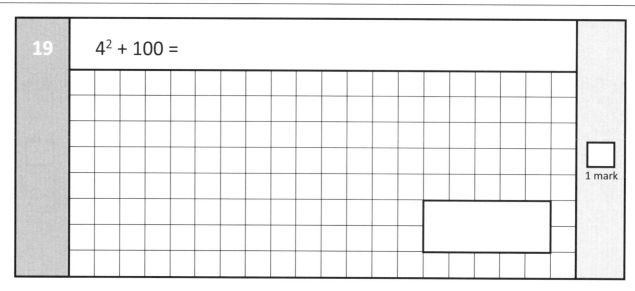

1 mark

20 $0.6 \div 100 =$

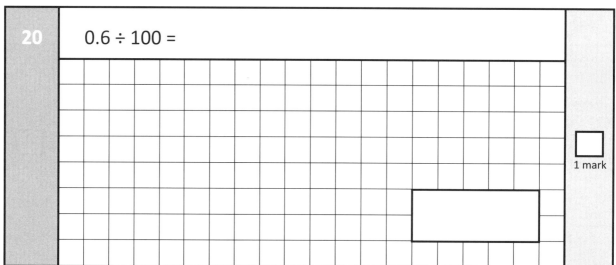

1 mark

21 $8 - 1.25 =$

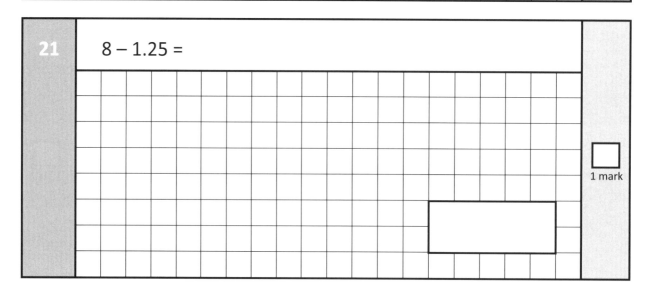

1 mark

21

MATHS
— YEAR 6 —

ARITHMETIC CHALLENGE

22

$$1{,}495 \div 13 =$$

1 mark

23

Show your method

$$\begin{array}{r} 7\ 8 \\ \times\quad 5\ 3 \\ \end{array}$$

2 marks

24

$$\frac{6}{8} + \frac{7}{8} =$$

1 mark

MATHS
— YEAR 6 —

ARITHMETIC CHALLENGE

25   15% of 1,600 =

1 mark

26   12 × 7.3 =

1 mark

27 $\dfrac{4}{5} - \dfrac{1}{10} =$

1 mark

MATHS
— YEAR 6 —

ARITHMETIC CHALLENGE

28

Show your method

3 9 1 0 1 4

2 marks

29

20% of 330 =

1 mark

30

Show your method

5 6 2 3
x   3 9

2 marks

24

ARITHMETIC CHALLENGE

31

$$2\frac{3}{8} + \frac{16}{32} =$$

1 mark

32

Show your method

	1	0	3	4
×			4	7

2 marks

33

$$\frac{4}{5} \div 4 =$$

1 mark

MATHS
— YEAR 6 —

TUTORS GUILD

ARITHMETIC CHALLENGE

34

$$\frac{3}{5} \times 165 =$$

1 mark

35

$$2\frac{1}{3} - \frac{3}{4} =$$

1 mark

36

$$(70 - 38) \div 8 =$$

1 mark

NUMBER, RATIO AND ALGEBRA CHALLENGE

WORKED EXAMPLES

1. Find the number that is exactly halfway between 5.1 and 5.8

5.8 – 5.1 = 0.7 *0.7 ÷ 2 = 0.36* *5.1 + 0.35 = 5.45*	**HINT:** First, work out the difference between the two numbers. Divide this by 2 to find half the difference. Add this amount to the lower number.

2. Coloured counters are put into a bag. There are 12 red counters and 4 green counters. What is the ratio of green to red counters? Give your answer in its simplest form.

green : red = 4 : 12 *simplest form = 1 : 3*	**HINT:** Read the question carefully to find out which order the numbers in your ratio should be in. Simplify your ratio by dividing each side by a common factor. Dividing by 4 will give you its simplest form.

3. Javid thinks of a number, then subtracts 7 from it. The number he ends up with is 45

a) Write this as a number sentence.

m – 7 = 45	**HINT:** Think about the calculation that is required to find the missing number. Choose a letter to represent the missing number, such as 'm'.

b) What number was Javid thinking of?

m – 7 = 45 *m = 45 + 7* *m = 52* *52 – 7 = 45*	**HINT:** Use your number sentence to work out the missing value. Use inverse operations to find out what *m* is. Put it back into your original number sentence to check.

NUMBER, RATIO AND ALGEBRA CHALLENGE

1. Fill in the missing numbers in these sentences.

One is done for you.

350   is 30 more than   .....320.....

....   is 30 less than   320

410   is 40 more than   ....

1 mark

2. If $r = 18$, what is $3r + 6$?

1 mark

NUMBER, RATIO AND ALGEBRA CHALLENGE

3. Each shape stands for a number.

■ + ■ + ■ = 57
■ + O + O + O = 88

Work out the value of each shape.

■ = ...   O = ...

2 marks

4. Some balls are put into a bag. Write the ratio of black balls to white balls in its simplest form.

....

1 mark

NUMBER, RATIO AND ALGEBRA CHALLENGE

5. These number cards have been muddled up.

a) Write the numbers in the correct order, from smallest to largest.

....

1 mark

b) Write the number on the cards above that is closest to 300

....

1 mark

c) Write the number on the cards above that is furthest from 300

....

1 mark

6. Max thinks of a number, f, and adds 9 to it. The answer is 25

a) Write this as a number sentence.

....

1 mark

b) What number was Max thinking of?

1 mark

NUMBER, RATIO AND ALGEBRA CHALLENGE

7. Luke was given these counters.
   Write the ratio of white counters to black counters.
   Give your answer in its simplest form.

....
1 mark

8. James wants to buy a new car. He looks at adverts in the newspaper.
   He wants to go to see the cars, starting with the cheapest.

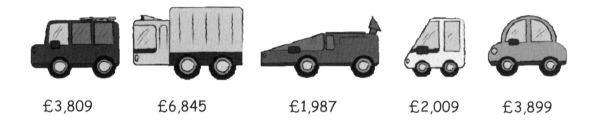

£3,809   £6,845   £1,987   £2,009   £3,899

Sort the amounts in order of price, starting with the lowest.

....
1 mark

NUMBER, RATIO AND ALGEBRA CHALLENGE

9. There are 190 buttons in a jar. 29 children each take six buttons from the jar for an art project. How many buttons are left in the jar?

2 marks

10. $5m - 6 = 69$
    Work out the value of m.

    $m =$ ....
    1 mark

11. A school craft club has 52 members. The ratio of boys to girls is $1 : 3$. How many boys and how many girls are in the club?

2 marks

12. Work out the value of s in this calculation.
    $135 \div s = 4.5$

    $s =$ ....
    1 mark

NUMBER, RATIO AND ALGEBRA CHALLENGE

13. A delivery company sells milk to customers for 95p per litre plus a delivery charge of 50p per order.

a) Write a formula that the delivery company could use to work out the total price for an order.

----

1 mark

b) One customer orders 5 litres of milk. What does she pay?

1 mark

14. In a sequence, the first term is 38 and the rule is 'subtract 7 from the previous term'. Write down the first eight terms of this sequence.

....

1 mark

15. Write in the three missing digits that will make this subtraction correct.

$$
\begin{array}{r}
7\ \square\ 8 \\
-\ 2\ 9\ \square \\
\hline
\square\ 8\ 1
\end{array}
$$

2 marks

33

NUMBER, RATIO AND ALGEBRA CHALLENGE

16. A snooker club has 60 members. The ratio of men to women is 4 : 1
    How many men and how many women attend the club?

.... men and .... women

2 marks

17. Here is a year written in Roman numerals: MMI

a) Write the year in numbers.

----
1 mark

b) Write the year 2010 in Roman numerals.

----
1 mark

18. Write the number that is halfway between 2.8 and 3.3

1 mark

NUMBER, RATIO AND ALGEBRA CHALLENGE

19. Simon's mum says that for every £1 he earns, she will give him £2.50. Simon does some jobs for his friends and family and earns £12

a) How much does Simon's mum give him?

1 mark

b) How much money does Simon have altogether?

1 mark

20. **Round 278,467 to:**

a) the nearest 10,000   ....

1 mark

b) the nearest 1,000   ....

1 mark

c) the nearest 10   ....

1 mark

NUMBER, RATIO AND ALGEBRA CHALLENGE

21. Freya is making some cakes. Here are the ingredients:
    200 g flour, 200 g sugar, 250 g butter, 10 g vanilla essence, 4 eggs

    This recipe makes 24 small cakes. Freya needs to make more than 24 cakes. She plans to scale up the recipe so that she uses 500 g of flour.

a) How many cakes will she be able to make?

1 mark

b) How much vanilla essence will she need?

1 mark

c) How many eggs will she need?

1 mark

22. Use your knowledge of place value to find these numbers.

a) Write the number that is 11 less than six million.

----
1 mark

b) Write the number that is ten thousand less than eight million.

----
1 mark

23. Three children share a pack of 114 cards in the ratio 1 : 3 : 2
    How many cards does each child get?

2 marks

GEOMETRY, MEASUREMENT AND STATISTICS CHALLENGE

WORKED EXAMPLES

1. Find the mean of these numbers: 45, 49, 32, 28

---

45 + 49 + 32 + 28 = 154

154 ÷ 4 = 38.5

HINT: First, add the values together.

Then divide your answer by the number of values you added together.

---

2. A triangle has angles of 36° and 101°. Calculate the size of the third angle.

36° + 101° = 137°

180° – 137° = 43°

HINT: The angles in a triangle add up to 180°, so you need to subtract the sum of the two angles you know from 180°.

First, add together the two angles you know, then subtract this answer from 180°.

MATHS
— YEAR 6 —

GEOMETRY, MEASUREMENT AND STATISTICS CHALLENGE

1. Name each shape.

A   B   C   D   E   F

A = ...   B = ...   C = ...

D = ...   E = ...   F = ...

3 marks

2. Write these measurements in order, from smallest to largest.

67 cm   1.45 m   156 cm   0.45 m   100 cm

....

1 mark

3. This diagram shows a shape on one side of a mirror line. Draw the reflection of the shape in the mirror line. Use a ruler.

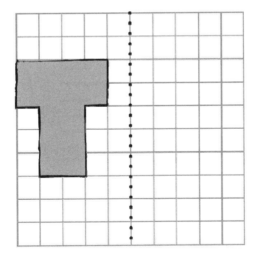

1 mark

GEOMETRY, MEASUREMENT AND STATISTICS CHALLENGE

4. What type of angle is this? Circle the correct description.

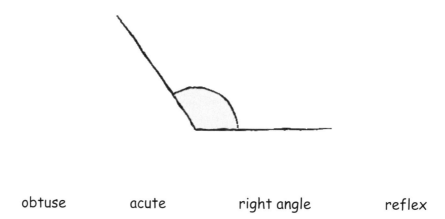

    obtuse   acute   right angle   reflex

1 mark

5. A mother uses this jug to measure the amount of milk needed for a baby's bottle.
   The baby needs 0.210 litres.
   Draw an arrow on the jug to show where she should pour to.

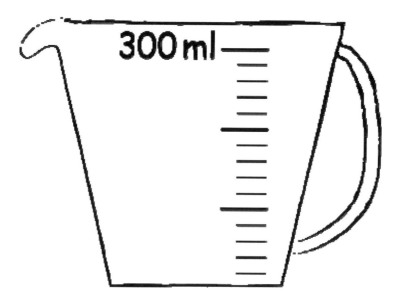

300 ml

1 mark

GEOMETRY, MEASUREMENT AND STATISTICS CHALLENGE

5. This table shows the average prices of houses in different areas of a town.

area	average house price
A	£308,950
B	£267,856
C	£195,789
D	£407,000

a) What is the difference between the average house prices in areas D and A?

1 mark

b) Dave buys one house in Area C and one in Area B. How much will he spend if he pays these average prices?

1 mark

7. A bottle holds 2 litres of liquid. Ernie pours 568 ml out of the bottle into a jug, and a further 0.789 litres into another jug. How much liquid is left in the bottle? Give your answer in litres.

2 marks

MATHS
— YEAR 6 —

GEOMETRY, MEASUREMENT AND STATISTICS CHALLENGE

8. Calculate the size of the angle marked *a* in this diagram.

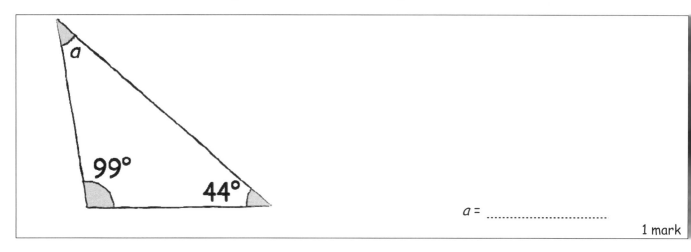

a = ...

1 mark

9. These potatoes weigh 1500 g. Mark this amount by drawing the missing pointer on the scales.

1 mark

GEOMETRY, MEASUREMENT AND STATISTICS CHALLENGE

10. A clock shows the time 03:30

a) Draw the hands on the clock to show this time.

1 mark

b) Write 3.30 pm in 24-hour time.

1 mark

11. This is part of a bus timetable from Highbridge to Curry Rivel.

Highbridge	13:05	13:25	13:45
Waterford	13:16	13:36	13:56
Hillingdon	13:32	13:52	14:12
Hinton	13:38	13:58	14:18
Curry Rivel	13:57	14:17	14:37

a) Jenny needs to be in Curry Rivel at 2.30 pm.
   What is the latest bus she could catch from Highbridge?

1 mark

b) How long does it take to get from Hillingdon to Curry Rivel?

1 mark

c) How long does the journey from Highbridge to Curry Rivel take?

1 mark

MATHS
— YEAR 6 —

GEOMETRY, MEASUREMENT AND STATISTICS CHALLENGE

12. The weight of a carrot is 22.5 g. The weight of a potato is 187.5 g. What is the total weight of two potatoes and three carrots?

2 marks

13. Each dot is 1 cm from the next. Join dots on the grid to make a shape that has an area of 6 cm² and a perimeter of 14 cm.

1 mark

14. A square is translated from Position A to Position B.

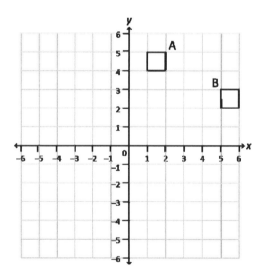

Complete this sentence:

The triangle has moved .... squares to the right and .... squares down.

1 mark

43

GEOMETRY, MEASUREMENT AND STATISTICS CHALLENGE

15. Look at this triangle.

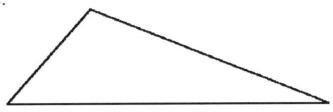

a) Using a ruler, measure the shortest side of this triangle. Give your answer in millimetres.

....
1 mark

b) Using a protractor, measure the largest angle.

....
1 mark

16. During the summer, Sam raised money for a charity.
This chart shows how much he collected.

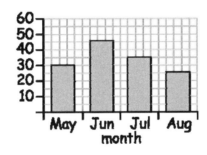

a) In which month did Sam collect more than £40?

....
1 mark

b) How much money did he collect in July?

....
1 mark

c) How much money did he collect in total in July and August?

....
1 mark

GEOMETRY, MEASUREMENT AND STATISTICS CHALLENGE

17. The kite on the grid is translated so that point A moves to point B.

a) Draw the kite in its new position. Use a ruler.

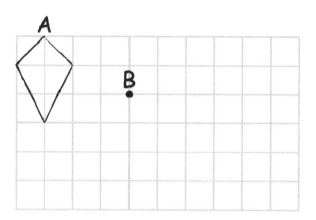

1 mark

b) Complete this sentence.

The kite has moved ....squares to the right and .... squares down.

1 mark

18. Owen buys six cans of drink. He pays with a £5 note. This is his change.

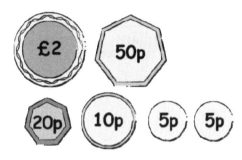

What is the cost of one can of drink?

2 marks

GEOMETRY, MEASUREMENT AND STATISTICS CHALLENGE

19. A parallelogram has two sets of parallel sides. You can show this on a diagram using pairs of arrows like this. On the first pair of parallel lines, draw a single arrow. On the next pair of parallel lines, draw two arrows.

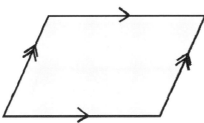

Mark the parallel lines on these shapes in the same way.
If a shape does not have any parallel lines, put a cross next to it.

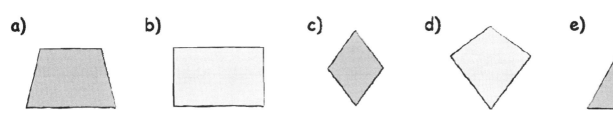

a)   b)   c)   d)   e)

2 marks

20. A school has a playground and a football pitch. The playground is 8,736 square metres. The football pitch is 105 metres long and 78 metres wide. How much larger is the area of the playground than the area of the football pitch?

2 marks

GEOMETRY, MEASUREMENT AND STATISTICS CHALLENGE

21. Write down the coordinates of the vertices of this trapezium.

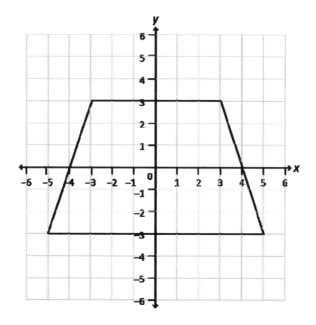

(,)   (,)   (,)   (,)

2 marks

22. Find the mean of these five values: 18   26   16   34   41

1 mark

GEOMETRY, MEASUREMENT AND STATISTICS CHALLENGE

23. The table shows how an insulated cup of boiling water cools over a 40-minute period.

time	9:00	9:10	9:20	9:30	9:40
temperature of water (°C)	100	90	75	60	40

a) Plot these temperatures onto the graph below.

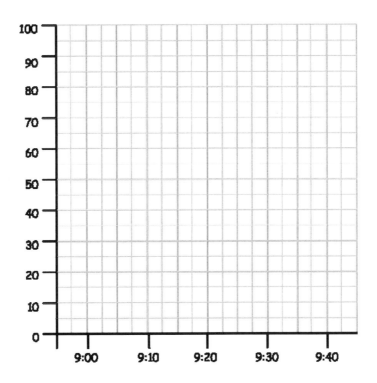

1 mark

b) Write a title and labels for the axes on your graph.

1 mark

1 DIAGNOSTIC (TOPIC TEST)

1. Circle a number in each row to show how confident you feel about the following areas of maths.

	low confidence ⟷ high confidence
Reading numbers	1 2 3 4 5 6 7 8 9 10
Adding up and subtracting	1 2 3 4 5 6 7 8 9 10
Multiplying and dividing	1 2 3 4 5 6 7 8 9 10
Using fractions, decimals and percentages	1 2 3 4 5 6 7 8 9 10
Using formulas	1 2 3 4 5 6 7 8 9 10
Finding the next number in a sequence	1 2 3 4 5 6 7 8 9 10
Reading scales	1 2 3 4 5 6 7 8 9 10
Choosing appropriate units	1 2 3 4 5 6 7 8 9 10
Working with time	1 2 3 4 5 6 7 8 9 10
Finding the areas and perimeters of shapes	1 2 3 4 5 6 7 8 9 10
Finding the volumes of shapes	1 2 3 4 5 6 7 8 9 10
Recognising 2D and 3D shapes	1 2 3 4 5 6 7 8 9 10
Measuring and working out angles	1 2 3 4 5 6 7 8 9 10
Using coordinate grids	1 2 3 4 5 6 7 8 9 10
Reading tables	1 2 3 4 5 6 7 8 9 10
Reading graphs and charts	1 2 3 4 5 6 7 8 9 10
Working out averages	1 2 3 4 5 6 7 8 9 10

2. List two things in maths that you are good at.

----

3. List two things in maths that you find difficult.

----

2 PLACE VALUE (TOPIC TEST)

1. Order these numbers from smallest to largest:

   989   1,045   898   998   1,005   888

   ....

   1 mark

2. Write a 6-digit number larger than five hundred thousand.   ....

   1 mark

3. Order these numbers from smallest to largest:

   3.678   2.078   2.909   3.001   2.990

   ....

   1 mark

4. Look at this number: 3,097,145

a) Write the digit that is in the ten thousands column.   ....

   1 mark

b) Write the number that is 900 more than this number.   ....

   1 mark

c) Write the number that is six thousand less than this number.   ....

   1 mark

d) Write the number that would be added to 3,097,145 to make 4,000,000

   > **HINT:** Start with the 1s column and work out what number you would need to add to the 5 to give you 0
   >
   > Work to the left, remembering to think about any digits you have carried over to the next column.

   2 marks

5. Write the number that is 5 tenths less than 98.867   ....

   2 marks

MATHS
— YEAR 6 —

3 ROUNDING (TOPIC TEST)

1. Round 6,083,457 to:

a) the nearest 10

....

1 mark

b) the nearest 100

....

1 mark

c) the nearest 1,000

....

1 mark

d) the nearest 10,000

....

1 mark

e) the nearest 100,000

....

1 mark

2. Round each of these numbers as instructed.

a) 16.8 to the nearest whole number

....

1 mark

b) 179.35 to the nearest whole number

....

1 mark

c) 24.87 to one decimal place

....

1 mark

d) 99.93 to one decimal place

....

1 mark

e) 13.986 to one decimal place

....

1 mark

51

4 ESTIMATING (TOPIC TEST)

1. Estimate the answer to each calculation.

a) 2,976 + 1,043 ≈

b) 575 – 189 ≈

....

1 mark

....

1 mark

2. Fred conducted a traffic survey for 2 hours outside his house. He put his results into a table.

cars	vans	motorbikes	campervans	lorries	buses
321	87	56	32	188	28

a) Estimate how many cars and vans drove past during the traffic survey. Show your working out.

2 marks

b) Estimate how many lorries, buses and motorbikes drove past during the traffic survey. Show your working out.

2 marks

c) Estimate how many cars and lorries drove past during the traffic survey. Show your working out.

2 marks

d) Estimate how many vehicles drove past during the traffic survey. Show your working out.

2 marks

5 ADDITION (TOPIC TEST)

1. Use your knowledge of place value to help you add these numbers mentally.

a) 10,678 + 6,211 = ...

1 mark

b) 832,789 + 164,332 = ...

1 mark

2. Complete these additions.

a)
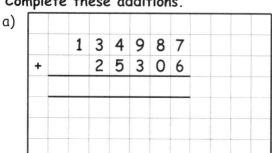

1 mark

b)
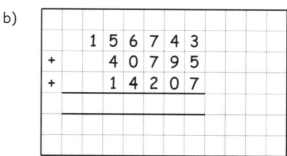

2 marks

3. On day 1 of a three-day festival, there were 11,765 guests. On day 2, there were 6,300 more guests than on day 1. On day 3, there were 25,900 guests.

a) How many guests were there in total on day 1 and day 3? Show your working out.

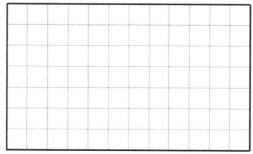

1 mark

HINT: Write out your addition on the squared paper. Make sure you think carefully about place value and line up the numbers correctly.

Start from the 1s column and work to the left. Remember to write any carried digits underneath the answer line.

b) How many guests were there in total on day 1 and day 2? Show your working out.

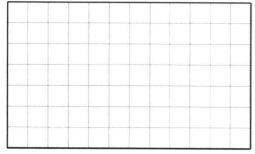

2 marks

c) How many guests were there in total over all three days? Show your working out.

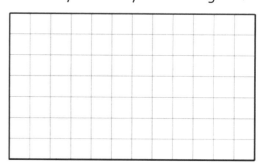

2 marks

6 SUBTRACTION (TOPIC TEST)

1. Use your knowledge of place value to help you subtract these numbers mentally.

a) 5,789 – 2,222 = ...

1 mark

b) 28,965 – 7,533 = ...

1 mark

c) 987,432 – 876,401 = ...

1 mark

d) 897,486 – 564,465 = ...

1 mark

2. Complete these subtractions.

a)

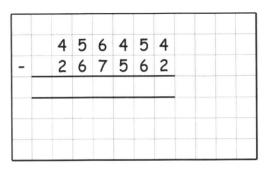

```
    4 5 6 4 5 4
-   2 6 7 5 6 2
```

1 mark

b)

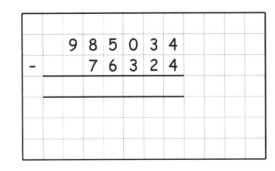

```
    9 8 5 0 3 4
-     7 6 3 2 4
```

1 mark

3. Simon collects stamps. He has 11,906 in total.

a) Simon has duplicates of 1,708 stamps. How many different stamps does he have?

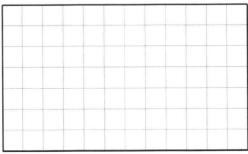

1 mark

b) Simon sells 673 stamps to one person and 396 to another. How many stamps are left?

2 marks

4. Aliysha is flying from Manchester airport to Valencia. After flying for an hour, the pilot says they have travelled 792 km out of a total distance of 1,564 km.

How far do they still have to travel? Show your working out.

....

1 mark

MATHS
— YEAR 6 —

7 MULTIPLES AND FACTORS (TOPIC TEST)

1. In each apple on the trees below, write a factor of the number in the tree.

a)

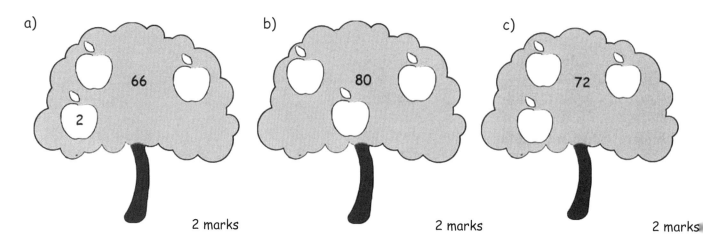

66

2

2 marks

b)

80

2 marks

c)

72

2 marks

2. Circle all of the prime numbers in the table below.

1	2	3	4	5	6	7	8	9	10
11	12	13	14	15	16	17	18	19	20
21	22	23	24	25	26	27	28	29	30

2 marks

3. Sort these numbers into the Venn diagram below: 17, 32, 40, 56, 70, 80, 92
Write any numbers that are not multiples of 8 or 10 outside the circles.

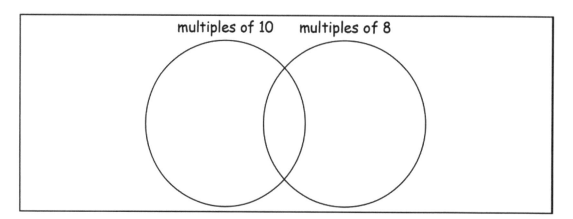

multiples of 10   multiples of 8

2 marks

55

3 SQUARES AND CUBES (TOPIC TEST)

1. The number 49 is a square number. Explain how you know this.

....

....

1 mark

2. The number 216 is a cube number. Explain how you know this.

....

....

1 mark

3. Use your knowledge of square and cube numbers to work out the answers to these calculations.

a) $6^2 + 9^2 =$

> **HINT:** Write out the calculation in full:
> $6 \times 6 + 9 \times 9$
> Remember to multiply first, then add.
>
> 2 marks

b) $5^3 + 6^3 =$

2 marks

c) $7^3 - 4^2 =$

2 marks

d) $9^3 - 8^2 =$

2 marks

9 MULTIPLICATION (TOPIC TEST)

1. Use your knowledge of place value to help you solve these calculations mentally.

a) 345 × 100 = ...

1 mark

b) 509 × 1,000 = ...

1 mark

c) 9,867 × 100 = ...

1 mark

d) 1,308 × 1,000 = ...

1 mark

2. Use short multiplication to complete these calculations.

a) 9,504 × 8 =

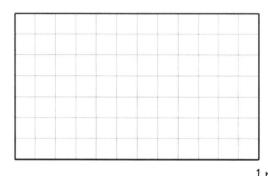

1 mark

b) 3,412 × 7 =

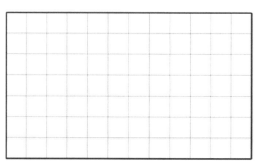

1 mark

3. Use long multiplication to complete these calculations.

HINT: Line up the digits carefully. First, multiply the top number by the 10s in the bottom number. Remember to write a 0 in the 1s column. Then multiply the top number by the 1s in the bottom number. Finally, add up the two numbers to find your answer.

a) 70 × 73 =

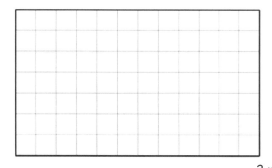

2 marks

b) 832 × 26 =

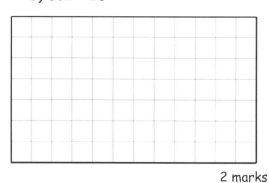

2 marks

10 DIVISION (TOPIC TEST)

1. Use your knowledge of multiplication facts to help you solve these divisions.

a) $45 \div 5 =$

1 mark

b) $56 \div 8 =$ ....

1 mark

2. Use short division to solve these calculations. Give any remainders as decimals.

a) $1,473 \div 6 =$

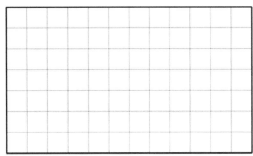

1 mark

b) $2,394 \div 7 =$

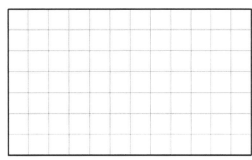

1 mark

3. Use long division to solve these calculations. Give any remainders as whole numbers.

a) $6,084 \div 24 =$

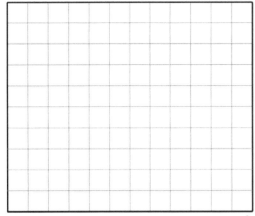

2 marks

b) $6,603 \div 31 =$

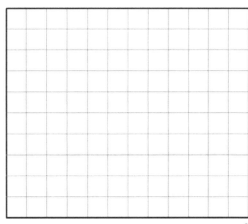

2 marks

4. A sweet shop sells large jars that contain 2,058 sweets. Mrs Tucker buys a jar and divides the sweets into bags to give to children at the school fair. She wants to put 14 sweets in each bag. How many bags will she be able to make?

HINT: Use long division. Write out the first few multiples of 14 first. Start with the first two digits of 2,058 and work to the right, subtracting multiples as you go.

2 marks

MATHS
— YEAR 6 —

11 ORDER OF OPERATIONS (TOPIC TEST)

1. Complete these calculations. Think carefully about the order in which you have to carry out the operations.

a) 16 × 5 + 8 =

1 mark

b) 30 × 15 – 27 =

1 mark

c) 56 ÷ 8 + 97 =

1 mark

d) 27 + (7 × 6) =

1 mark

2. Max has 6 bags of conkers. There are 12 conkers in each bag. He also has 38 more conkers in a box. How many conkers does he have altogether?

HINT: Write an equation for working out the number of marbles Max has. Remember to do the multiplication before you add.

2 marks

3. Padma has 9 sheets of stickers. Each sheet has 16 stickers. She gives away 25 stickers. How many stickers does she have left?

2 marks

4. Oscar has 63 toy animals. He divides them equally into 9 boxes. He is then given 27 more animals and divides these equally into the same 9 boxes. How many animals are in each box now?

2 marks

12 PROPER FRACTIONS (TOPIC TEST)

1. For each shape below, write the fraction that is shaded and give an equivalent fraction.

a)

fraction shaded =

....

equivalent fraction =

....

2 marks

b)

fraction shaded =

....

equivalent fraction =

....

2 marks

c)

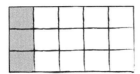

fraction shaded =

....

equivalent fraction =

....

2 marks

2. Write each of these fractions in its simplest form.

a) $\dfrac{12}{36}$ =

....

1 mark

b) $\dfrac{21}{84}$ =

....

1 mark

c) $\dfrac{36}{66}$ =

....

1 mark

d) $\dfrac{8}{60}$ =

....

1 mark

13 FRACTIONS GREATER THAN 1 (TOPIC TEST)

1. Convert these mixed numbers to improper fractions.

a) $3\frac{6}{9}$ =

1 mark

b) $5\frac{4}{8}$ =

1 mark

c) $9\frac{3}{5}$ =

1 mark

2. Convert these improper fractions to mixed numbers.

a) $\frac{35}{6}$ =

1 mark

b) $\frac{44}{7}$ =

1 mark

c) $\frac{51}{9}$ =

1 mark

3. Write a < or > sign between each pair of fractions to show which is bigger.

a) $\frac{5}{7}$ $\frac{4}{35}$

1 mark

b) $\frac{7}{8}$ $\frac{58}{64}$

1 mark

c) $1\frac{4}{9}$ $\frac{40}{27}$

1 mark

d) $\frac{70}{60}$ $2\frac{7}{12}$

1 mark

14 ADDING AND SUBTRACTING FRACTIONS (TOPIC TEST)

. Look at the fraction in the circles below, then write four equivalent fractions in the boxes around each one.

a)

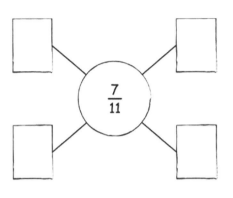

2 marks

b)

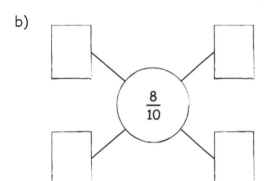

2 marks

2. Solve these fraction calculations. Give your answers as mixed numbers.

a) $\dfrac{5}{8} + \dfrac{7}{8} =$

HINT: If the denominators are the same, you can just add the numerators. If they are different, you need to find equivalent fractions with the same denominators.

2 marks

b) $\dfrac{12}{9} + \dfrac{2}{3} =$

2 marks

c) $3\dfrac{6}{7} - \dfrac{20}{14} =$

2 marks

15 MULTIPLYING FRACTIONS AND DECIMALS (TOPIC TEST)

1. Use your knowledge of place value to help you multiply these decimals.

a) $5.98 \times 100 = $ ....

1 mark

b) $0.05 \times 1{,}000 = $ ....

1 mark

2. Multiply these fractions by the whole numbers shown.

a) $5 \times \dfrac{6}{7} = $

1 mark

b) $14 \times \dfrac{1}{9} = $

1 mark

3. Multiply these decimals by the whole numbers shown.

a) $1.35 \times 9 = $

1 mark

b) $2.96 \times 5 = $

1 mark

4. Multiply these fractions. Give your answers in their simplest form.

a) $\dfrac{4}{7} \times \dfrac{8}{9} = $

2 marks

b) $\dfrac{11}{14} \times \dfrac{6}{8} = $

2 marks

6 DIVIDING FRACTIONS AND DECIMALS (TOPIC TEST)

. Use your knowledge of place value to help you solve these division calculations.

) $6.78 \div 10 =$ ....

1 mark

) $3.05 \div 100 =$ ....

1 mark

) $12.07 \div 1,000 =$ ....

1 mark

. Divide these proper fractions by the whole numbers shown.

a) $\dfrac{7}{13} \div 8 =$

1 mark

b) $\dfrac{9}{14} \div 7 =$

1 mark

c) $\dfrac{5}{18} \div 5 =$

1 mark

. Find the decimal equivalents of these fractions.

a) $\dfrac{12}{48} =$

2 marks

b) $\dfrac{18}{90} =$

2 marks

17 PERCENTAGES (TOPIC TEST)

1. Write these fractions as percentages:

a) $\dfrac{76}{100}$ = ...
1 mark

b) $\dfrac{7}{10}$ = ...
1 mark

2. Write these fractions as percentages.
   Remember to convert them to fractions out of 100 first.

a) $\dfrac{2}{5}$ = ...
1 mark

b) $\dfrac{13}{20}$ = ...
1 mark

c) $\dfrac{17}{25}$ = ...
1 mark

d) $\dfrac{42}{50}$ = ...
1 mark

3. 25 children are going on a school trip next week. 21 children have already paid for their tickets. What percentage of children still need to pay for their tickets?

HINT: First, subtract the number of children who have paid from the total number of children to find out how many have not paid. Write a fraction with this number as the numerator and the total number as the denominator. Find an equivalent fraction with the denominator 100.

1 mark

4. Solve these percentage calculations.

a) 25% of 220 =

1 mark

b) 37% of 110 =

2 marks

18 Equivalence (topic test)

1. Complete the table to show the equivalent percentages, decimals and fractions.

percentage	decimal	fraction
20%		
	0.64	
		$\dfrac{9}{25}$

6 marks

2. In Grove Park school, 70% of the pupils speak English as their first language.
   0.2 of the pupils have Polish as their first language and the remaining pupils speak a variety of other languages as their first language.

a) Write the decimal equivalent of children who have English as a first language.

HINT: Divide the percentage by 100

1 mark

b) What fraction of children have Polish as their first language?

1 mark

c) Write down the fraction of children that have another language (other than Polish or English) as their first language.

1 mark

d) Of the children who speak English as a first language, 35% of them also speak another language. What fraction of this group do not also speak a different language?

1 mark

19 RATIO (TOPIC TEST)

1. For each picture below, first write the ratio of plain shirts to striped shirts, then write the proportion of the shirts that are striped as a fraction.

a)

ratio = ...   proportion that are striped = ...

2 marks

b)

ratio = ...   proportion that are striped = ...

2 marks

c)

ratio = ...   proportion that are striped = ...

2 marks

2. £105 is divided between two children in the ratio of 3 : 7. How much does each child get?

2 marks

3. For every £1 that Freda earns washing cars, her mum gives her £2. At the end, Freda has a total of £54. How many cars did she wash?

HINT: To work out how much Freda earns per car, add together the amount she is paid plus the amount her mum gives her.

Divide the total amount by this to find out how many cars she washed.

2 marks

20 SCALE FACTORS (TOPIC TEST)

1. Below each shape, draw how it will look after being enlarged or reduced by the scale factor shown.

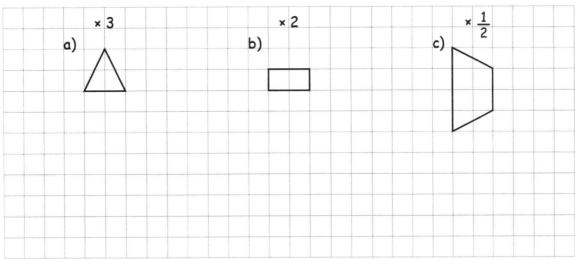

a) × 3

b) × 2

c) × $\frac{1}{2}$

3 marks

2. What is the scale factor of enlargement between the first rectangle and the second rectangle? The diagram is not to scale.

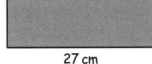

3 cm   27 cm

2 marks

3. A square has an area of 9 cm². It is enlarged and the new square has an area of 144 cm². What is the scale factor of enlargement?

HINT: If the area of the first square is 9 cm², the length of each side must be 3 cm². Use this method to work out the length of the sides of the new square. Then divide the new side length by the original side length to find the scale factor.

2 marks

4. A swimming pool measures 50 m by 70 m. It is drawn on to a plan with a scale factor of 500. What are the dimensions of the swimming pool on the plan? Give your answer in centimetres.

3 marks

21 SIMPLE FORMULAS (TOPIC TEST)

1. Fill in the missing numbers in these calculations.

a) 756 – .... = 406

1 mark

b) 9 × .... = 108

1 mark

c) 131 + ... = 269

1 mark

2. Find the values of the letters in each of these equations.

a) $5h + 8h = 32.5$

> **HINT:** Add $5h$ and $8h$. Divide both sides by the same number to get the h on its own.
>
> 1 mark

b) $35 + 8m = 83$

1 mark

c) $8w - 5 = 67$

1 mark

3. Solve these equations.

a) $(k - 315) \times 9 = 765$

2 marks

b) $(s + 315) \div 20 = 19$

2 marks

2 LINEAR SEQUENCES (TOPIC TEST)

. Complete each number sequence by filling in the missing number.

HINT: Work out the difference between one term and the next. Add this amount on to the term that comes before the one you don't know.

a) 9, 18, 27, ..., 45, 54

1 mark

b) 21, 28, 35, 42, ..., 56, 63

1 mark

. Identify the rule for each sequence and then write in the missing numbers.

a) 43, 47, 51, 55, ..., 63, ..., 71

Term-to-term rule: ....

3 marks

b) 98, 90, 82 , ..., 66, ... , 50

Term-to-term rule: ....

3 marks

3. Write the first six terms of the sequence that is being described.

first term: 17   term-to-term rule: add 9 to the previous term

.... , ... , ... , ... , ... , ...

2 marks

23 TWO UNKNOWNS (TOPIC TEST)

1. Find all the possible pairs of numbers for each equation and its rule.

a) $j + k = 32$ (where j and k are positive integers less than 20)

----
2 marks

b) $m + n = 56$ (where m and n are positive integers less than 31)

----
2 marks

c) $d - c = 15$ (where c and d are positive integers less than 21)

----
2 marks

2. There are four different jobs for children in each class in a school (librarian, sports captain, register monitor and snack monitor). There are five classes in the school (oak, hazel, rowan, sycamore and beech). How many children are needed to do each of the roles in the school and what are the combinations?

> **HINT:** To find the number of children needed, multiply the number of jobs by the number of classes.
>
> Then list all of the combinations in a table with each class in a different row and each job in a different column.

4 marks

MATHS
— YEAR 6 —

TUTORS GUILD

4 SCALES AND UNITS (TOPIC TEST)

1. Convert these measurements to the units given in the header of the table.

convert to ml	convert to m	convert to km	convert to kg
11.078 litres =	808 cm =	307 m =	1,056 g =
0.986 litres =	1,950 cm =	11,067 m =	10,011 g =

4 marks

2. Use this table to convert these measurements between imperial and metric units.

	length	weight	capacity
	1 mile ≈ 1.6 km	1 pound ≈ 400 g	1 pint ≈ 500ml
	1 inch ≈ 2.5 cm	1 ounce ≈ 30 g	

a) Approximately how many inches are there in 25 cm?

2 marks

b) Approximately how many pints is the same as 3 litres?

2 marks

c) Approximately how many grams are there in 12 ounces?

2 marks

25 WORKING WITH UNITS (TOPIC TEST)

1. Convert these amounts into pounds and pence.

a) 109p = ...   b) 84p = ...
                               1 mark   1 mark

c) 10,107p = ...   d) 201,100p = ...
                               1 mark   1 mark

2. Order these units of measurement from smallest to largest.

a) 67 m   67 cm   1.56 m   0.8 km   680 mm

   ....
                                                                                              2 marks

b) 3.9 kg   12 g   1.09 kg   208 g   110 g

   ....
                                                                                              2 marks

3. Susan is watering her garden. She has three watering cans that hold different amounts.
   She fills all three and uses them to water the garden.

   The first holds 14,986 ml, the second holds 11.678 litres and the third holds 8,765 ml.

   How much water does she use on the garden? Give your answer in litres.

   2 marks

6 TIME (TOPIC TEST)

. Write these Roman numerals as standard numbers.

) MMX = ...

1 mark

b) XXXV = ...

1 mark

. Convert these 24-hour times to 12-hour times and draw the hands on the clock faces.
Write am or pm next to the clock to show if it is morning or afternoon.

)

```
21:50
```

2 marks

•)

```
05:20
```

2 marks

)

```
13:15
```

2 marks

3. A clock on a computer shows 17:15
What time did it show 40 minutes earlier? Write your answer in 12-hour time.

> **HINT:** First subtract 15 minutes to get to 17:00. Then subtract the other 25 minutes.
>
> The time is in the afternoon because the hours are above 12, so remember to write pm after the time.
>
> 2 marks

MATHS
— YEAR 6 —

27 PERIMETER (TOPIC TEST)

1. Write the perimeters of this square and rectangle. Show your working out.

a)

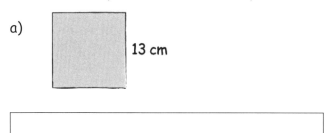

13 cm

b)

15 cm

18 cm

1 mark

1 mark

2. Write the length of the missing sides on each compound shape and then find its perimeter.

a)

10 m

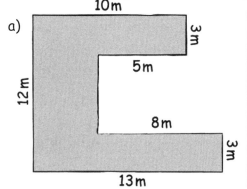

3 m

5 m

12 m

8 m

3 m

13 m

HINT: To find the missing side lengths, divide the shape up into smaller shapes and look for sides that have the same lengths.

2 marks

b)

2 cm

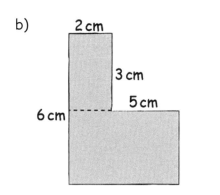

3 cm

5 cm

6 cm

2 marks

c)

9 cm

2 cm

3 cm

3 cm

4 marks

75

8 AREA OF A RECTANGLE (TOPIC TEST)

. Multiply these numbers together as quickly as you can.

) 12 × 9 = ...

1 mark

b) 6 × 100 = ...

1 mark

) 7 × 8 = ...

1 mark

d) 2.5 × 8 = ...

1 mark

. Find the area of this rectangle.

21 cm

11 cm

2 marks

. Laila is setting up a cake stall on three tables. She wants to work out how much space she has altogether for her cakes. Work out the area of each table and then find the total area of the tables. Give your answers in square metres.

table	width	length	area
1	1.2 m	3 m	
2	0.6 m	0.8 m	
3	1.5 m	1.5 m	

total area of tables =

4 marks

29 AREAS OF OTHER SHAPES (TOPIC TEST)

1. Find the areas of the triangles described.

a) A triangle with a base of 9 cm and a perpendicular height of 13 cm.

HINT: The area of a triangle is half its base multiplied by its height.

2 marks

b) A triangle with a base of 6.5 cm and a perpendicular height of 5 cm.

2 marks

2. What is the area of this triangle?

15 cm

42 cm

2 marks

3. Find the areas of these parallelograms.

a) A parallelogram with a length of 12 cm and a perpendicular height of 8 cm.

2 marks

b) A parallelogram with a length of 31 cm and a perpendicular height of 12 cm.

2 marks

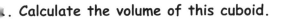

MATHS
— YEAR 6 —

30 VOLUME (TOPIC TEST)

1. Calculate the volume of this cuboid.

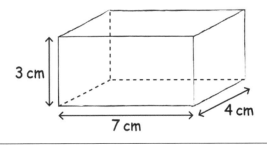

3 cm

7 cm

4 cm

> **HINT:** The volume of a cuboid is found by multiplying its length by its width and height.
>
> 2 marks

2. A cuboid has a length of 13 cm, a width of 5 cm and a height of 9 cm. What is the volume of the cuboid?

2 marks

3. A cuboid has a length of 21 cm, a width of 18 cm and a height of 11 cm. What is the volume of the cuboid?

2 marks

4. A cuboid has a length of 25 cm, a width of 27 cm and a height of 20 cm. What is the volume of the cuboid?

2 marks

5. A cube has sides measuring 3.5 m. What is the volume of the cube?

2 marks

31 2D SHAPES (TOPIC TEST)

1. Write the name of each shape below, stating whether it is regular or irregular.

   HINT: Regular shapes have all sides the same length and all angles the same size.

	name of shape	regular or irregular?

a)

....

2 mark:

b)

....

2 mark:

c)

....

2 mark:

d)

....

2 marks

e)

....

2 marks

32 3D SHAPES (TOPIC TEST)

1. Name each shape.

a)

b)

c)

--------------------------------- --------------------------------- ---------------------------------
1 mark   1 mark   1 mark

2. Complete this table with the numbers of faces, vertices and edges for each shape.

shape	faces	vertices	edges
tetrahedron			
hexagonal prism			

6 marks

3. This is the net for a 3D shape. Name the shape.

HINT: Two of the faces are pentagons. Imagine folding up the net so you can picture where the faces would be in the shape.

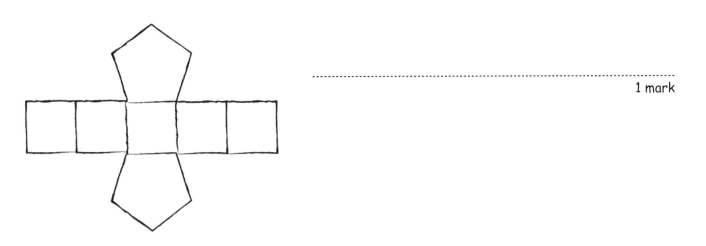

----

1 mark

33 ANGLES (TOPIC TEST)

1. Measure each angle and write its size on the diagram. Then write whether it is acute, obtuse, reflex or a right angle.

a)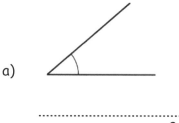

....
2 marks

b)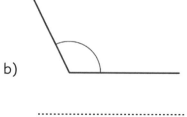

....
2 marks

2. Work out the missing angle in each diagram.

a)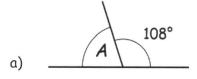

A = ...
1 mark

b)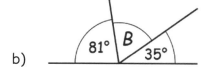

B = ...
1 mark

c)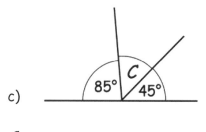

C = ...
1 mark

d)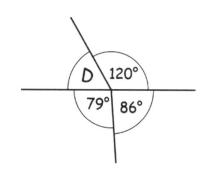

D = ...
1 mark

3. Use your knowledge of circles to answer these questions.

a) The diameter of a circle is 32 cm. What is its radius?

----
1 mark

b) The radius of a wheel is 34 cm. What is its diameter?

----
1 mark

34 TRANSFORMATIONS (TOPIC TEST)

1. Look at the grid and write the coordinates of each cross.

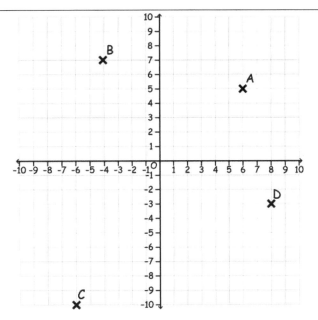

A = ...

B = ...

C = ...

D = ...

1 mark

2. Draw the reflection of each shape below.

a)

b)

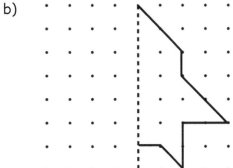

3 marks   3 marks

3. Translate this shape 4 squares to the right and 3 squares up.
   Write the coordinates of the new positions of points A, B and C.

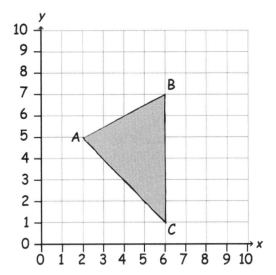

A = ...

B = ...

C = ...

3 marks

35 TABLES (TOPIC TEST)

1. This table shows 200 children's favourite flavours of ice cream. Fill in the gaps in the table. Show your working out in the box below.

favourite flavour	number of children	percentage of children
strawberry		20%
vanilla	50	
chocolate		30%
mint	30	
other		

HINT: First, fill in the blanks in the first four rows. To fill in the blanks in the last row, add up each column. Subtract the total number of children from 200, and subtract the total percentage from 100%.

6 marks

2. Look at this bus timetable and answer the questions.

Street	10:40	11:10	11:40	12:10	12:40
Glastonbury	10:55	11:25	11:55	12:25	12:55
Wells	11:18	11:48	12:18	12:48	13:18
Pilton	11:50	12:20	12:50	13:20	13:50

a) How long does it take to get from Street to Pilton? ....

1 mark

b) How long does it take to get from Street to Wells? ....

1 mark

c) How often do buses leave Wells for Pilton? ....

1 mark

d) Sian wants to be in Wells for 12:30. What is the latest bus she can take from Street?

....

1 mark

36 CHARTS (TOPIC TEST)

. Look at this chart and answer the questions.

a) Write a title that could go on the vertical axis.

.... 1 mark

b) Write a title that could go on the horizontal axis.

.... 1 mark

c) How many children liked green best?

.... 1 mark

Favourite colours of children in a school

(Bar chart: y-axis from 0 to 80; bars — blue 70, red 55, green 40, orange 15, white 10, yellow 10, pink 5)

d) How many children were asked their favourite colour in total?

> **HINT:** Look at the height of the first bar. Read across to the y-axis to see how many people this represents, then do the same for the remaining bars.
> Add all of these numbers together to find out the total number of children asked.
> 2 marks

2. Look at this pie chart and answer the questions.

How children travel to school

(Pie chart with sectors: taxi, car, cycle, walk, bus)

a) Approximately what percentage of children travel by car?

.... 1 mark

b) Circle the sector that represents the children who walk to school.
1 mark

c) Approximately what percentage of children cycle or travel by taxi? .... 1 mark

d) Approximately what percentage of children walk or take the bus? .... 1 mark

e) Approximately what percentage of children travel by bus? .... 1 mark

37 LINE GRAPHS (TOPIC TEST)

1. This line graph shows the temperatures on a Thursday in June.

a) What was the temperature at 22:00?

----
                                                    1 mark

b) What time was the highest temperature?
   What was it?

----
                                                    2 marks

c) What time was the lowest temperature?
   What was it?

----
                                                    2 marks

d) How many degrees was the difference between the highest and lowest temperatures?

                                                    1 mark

e) By how many degrees did the temperature drop between 12:00 and 20:00?

                                                    2 marks

f) What was the difference between the temperature at 06:00 and 10:00?

                                                    2 marks

38 MEAN AVERAGES (TOPIC TEST)

. Find the mean of each set of values. Give your answers to 1 decimal place.

a) 12 cm 17 cm 11 cm 19 cm 21 cm 5 cm

1 mark

b) 38 ml 289 ml 145 m 189 ml

1 mark

c) 9p 56p 85p 16p 49p

1 mark

d) 75 69 104 67 119 88 54 89 89

1 mark

e) 1,001 989 1,114 1,021 1,038 967 901

1 mark

f) £1.89 199p £2.05 £0.98 89p £1.04

2 marks

2. These are the marks of five children who took a test: 16   19   ?   26   19
One child didn't want to share their mark with the class. If the mean mark was 19, what was the missing mark?

HINT: Multiply the mean by the number of values to find the total number of marks for all five children.

Subtract the values you know to find the missing mark.

3 marks

PRACTICE PAPERS

On the following pages, you will find a set of practice papers modelled on the sample assessment material and past papers provided by the government. It comprises an arithmetic test and two reasoning tests. The booklet includes space for your student's answers.

If you want to see how your student performs in test conditions, provide a quiet working environment, adhere to the timings given on each paper and answer questions relating to the practicalities of the test only. None of the tests require a calculator.

PAPER 1: ARITHMETIC

The arithmetic test comprises 36 questions, worth a total of 40 marks.

The test should take 30 minutes to complete.

The student will encounter context-free questions on mathematical operations.

The answers for the arithmetic paper can be found on page 138.

PAPERS 2 AND 3: REASONING

There are two reasoning tests. Each test comprises 20 questions and is worth a total of 35 marks.

Each test should take 40 minutes to complete.

The student will encounter both contextual and context-free questions on number, ratio, algebra, measurement, geometry and statistics.

The answers for the reasoning papers can be found on pages 139–141.

MATHS
— YEAR 6 —

Mathematics
Paper 1: arithmetic

Instructions

Before you start

Make sure you have a pen or pencil.

You are **not** allowed to use a calculator.

Questions and answers

Do your working out on the grid. Put your final answer in the box.

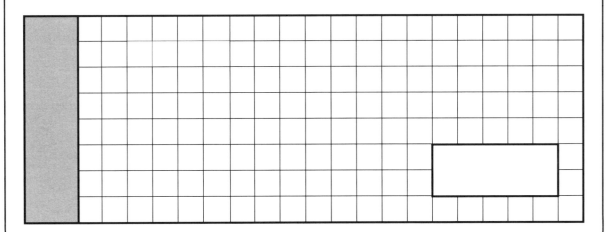

Marks
The number at the side of the page tells you the maximum number of marks for each question.

1

903 + 100 =

1 mark

2

243 × 2 =

1 mark

3

5.6 + 0.2 =

1 mark

4 32 × 3 =

1 mark

5 1,067 + 698 =

1 mark

6 42 ÷ 7 =

1 mark

7   874 − 7 =

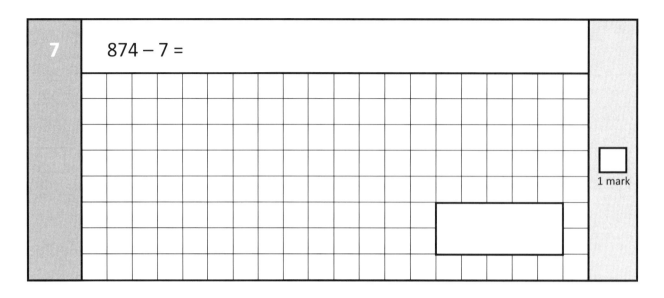

1 mark

8   5.6 + 0.04 =

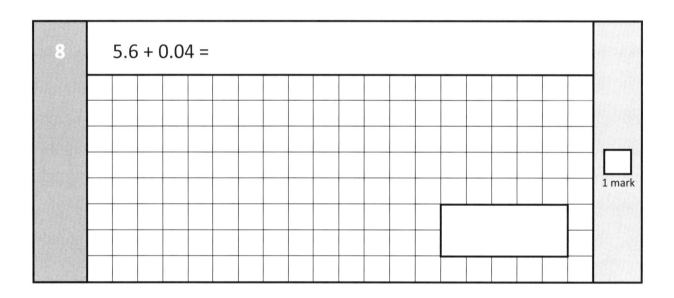

1 mark

9   6 × 3 × 9 =

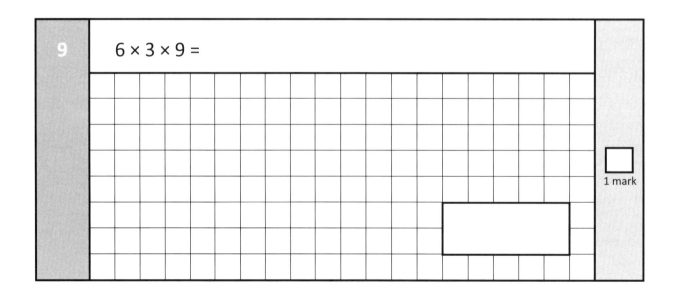

1 mark

10 $\dfrac{6}{7} - \dfrac{2}{7} =$

1 mark

11 $640 \div 8 =$

1 mark

12 $4.56 \times 100 =$

1 mark

13

$7^2 =$

1 mark

14

$75{,}000 - 500 =$

1 mark

15

$1{,}000 \times 100 =$

1 mark

16 1,800 ÷ 12 =

1 mark

17 40% of 2,400 =

1 mark

18 1.39 × 8 =

1 mark

19 $\dfrac{2}{11} + \dfrac{6}{11} =$

1 mark

20 4,804 + 7,061 =

1 mark

21 8,754 ÷ 6 =

1 mark

22

15 − 8.045 =

1 mark

23

Show your method

```
      6 3
  ×   2 6
```

2 marks

24

19.3 − 9.69 =

1 mark

25

Show your method

1 1 2 9 3 7

2 marks

26

$$\frac{1}{3} \times \frac{1}{9} =$$

1 mark

27

85% of 380 =

1 mark

28   367,963 + 53,998 =

1 mark

29

Show your method

| | | 7 | 3 | 8 |
| × | | | 7 | 4 |

2 marks

30 $24 \times 2\frac{1}{2} =$

1 mark

31 $52 - 6 \times 8 =$

1 mark

32 $\dfrac{6}{8} \div 2 =$

1 mark

33 $1\dfrac{4}{5} - \dfrac{6}{10} =$

1 mark

34

Show your method

4 1 2 4 1 9

2 marks

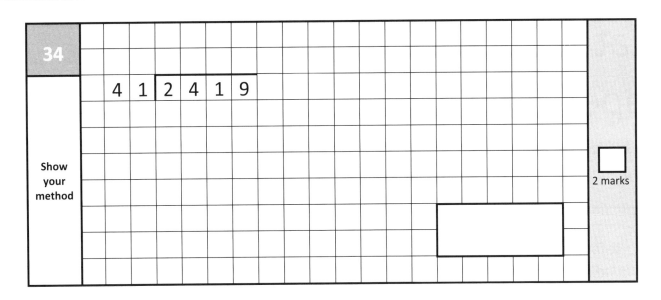

35

$$\frac{2}{6} \times \frac{11}{24} =$$

1 marks

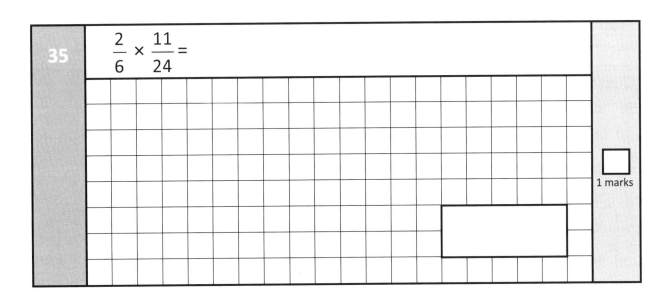

36

$$\frac{5}{8} \div 2 =$$

1 marks

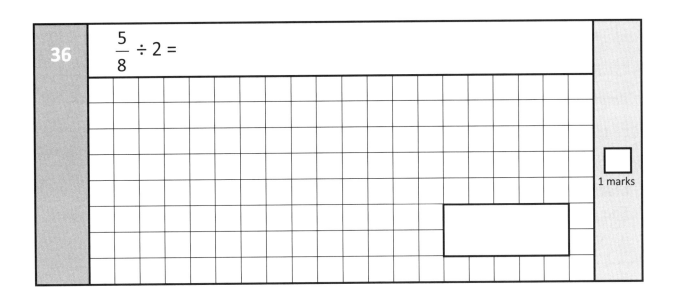

MATHS
— YEAR 6 —

Mathematics
Paper 2: reasoning

Instructions

Before you start

Make sure you have a pen, pencil, rubber, ruler, angles measurer or protractor and a mirror.

You are **not** allowed to use a calculator or tracing paper.

Questions and answers

If you need to do working out, you can use the space around the question.

Some questions have a method box like this:

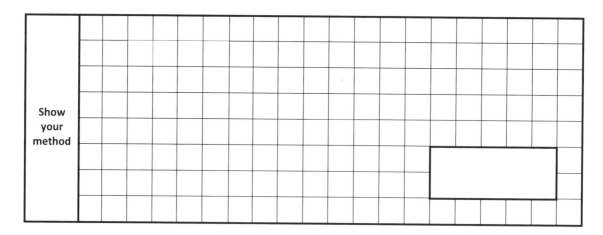

For these questions you may get a mark for showing your method.

Marks

The number at the side of the page tells you the maximum number of marks for each question.

1 Look at these numbers.

765   805   678   798   815

Write the number that is closest to 700

1 mark

Write the number that is furthest from 700

1 mark

2 In the circles below, write a multiple that belongs to each set.

One has been done for you.

numbers from 1 to 99	multiple of 10	(50)
numbers from 101 to 199	multiple of 30	◯
numbers from 201 to 299	multiple of 50	◯
numbers from 301 to 399	multiple of 70	◯

2 marks

3 Write the three missing digits to make this addition correct.

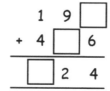

```
      1  9  □
  +   4  □  6
  ─────────────
      □  2  4
```

2 mark

4 This graph shows the temperature in six cities one day in December.

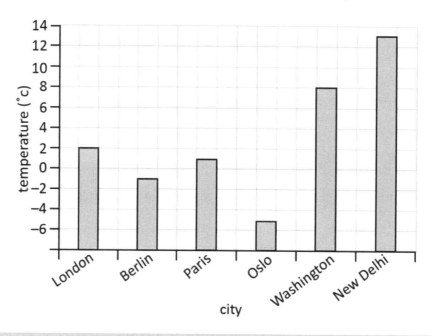

In which city was the temperature 6 degrees lower than in Paris?

_____

1 mark

What was the difference between the temperature in New Delhi and the temperature in Oslo?

| °C |

1 mark

5 Write each number in the correct place on this Venn diagram.

2   7   8   14   19   27   46   64   71   89   125

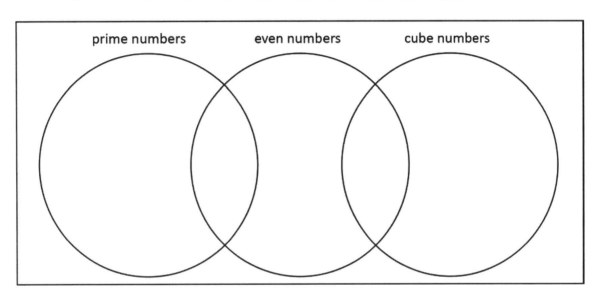

2 marks

6 Here are some shapes that have been divided into equal sections.

Some of the sections are shaded in each shape.

For each shape, write the ratio of shaded sections to white sections in its simplest form.

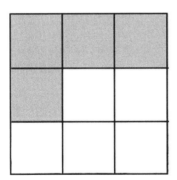

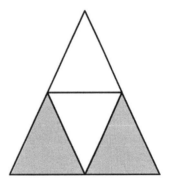

_____   _____

2 marks

7 Put these cars in order of price, starting with the lowest price.

£78,500   £101,867   £99,705   £101,890   £110,689

One has been done for you.

lowest   **highest**

£78,500   _____   _____   _____   _____

1 mar

8 Circle two numbers that add together to equal 0.45

0.15   0.2   0.1   0.25   0.035

1 mark

105

9 4 elephant keyrings cost £3.44

3 elephant keyrings and 1 tiger keyring cost £3.33

What is the cost of 1 tiger keyring?

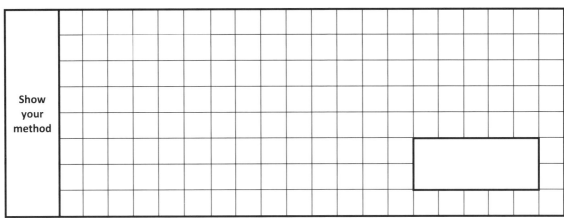

Show your method

2 marks

Each diagram below is divided into equal sections.

Shade $\frac{3}{5}$ of each of the shapes below.

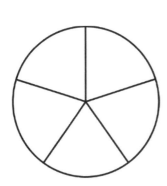
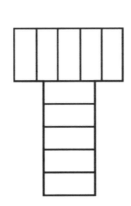
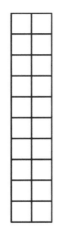

2 marks

11 What is 346 minutes in hours and minutes?

_____

1 mar

12 Look at the time on the clock face opposite.
The clock is 13 minutes slow.

What is the correct time in 24-hour time?

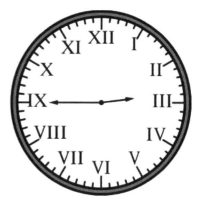

_____

1 mar

13 A company makes gift cards and sells them in boxes.
It uses this formula to work out how much to charge for each box of gift cards:

cost = number of cards × 76p + £1.20 for the box

Write a number sentence for this, if the cost is *C* and number of cards is *n*.

_____

1 mark

How much will a box of 10 gift cards cost?

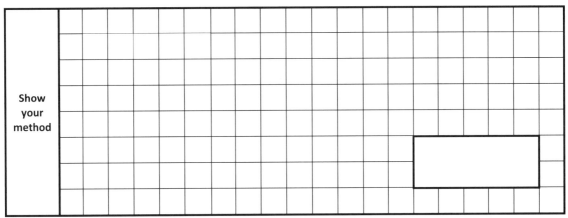

Show
your
method

1 mark

Coby buys a box of gift cards for £13.36

Use the formula to calculate how many gift cards there are in Coby's box.

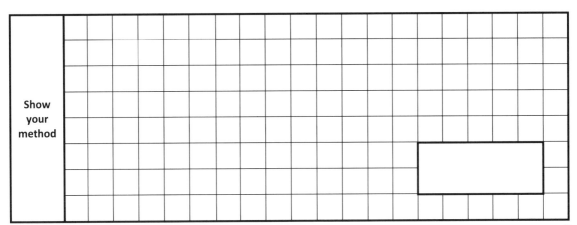

Show
your
method

2 marks

14 A packet contains 1.8 kg of breakfast cereal.
Every day, Oscar uses 40 g for his breakfast.

How many days will the packet of breakfast cereal last him?

Show your method

2 mark

15 Rafael builds the foundation of a wall that is 240 cm long. He uses 8 identical bricks to make his wall.

He needs to make the wall 330 cm long.

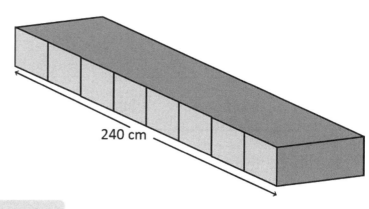

240 cm

How many more bricks will he need?

Show your method

1 mark

16 Write all the common multiples of 3 and 7 that are less than 70

_____

1 mark

17 Write the missing value to make this pair of fractions equivalent.

$$\frac{\Box}{6} = \frac{20}{30}$$

1 mark

18 Write the two missing digits to make this long multiplication correct.

$$
\begin{array}{r}
6\ \square \\
\times\ \ \square\ 5 \\
\hline
1\ 8\ 6\ 0 \\
3\ 1\ 0 \\
\hline
2\ 1\ 7\ 0 \\
\end{array}
$$

2 mark

19 A triangle with points P, Q and R has been drawn on this coordinate grid.

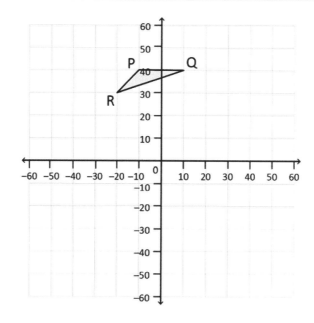

Reflect the triangle in the *x*-axis and write the new coordinates for points P, Q and R below.

P = _____   Q = _____   R = _____

1 mark

20 This thermometer shows a temperature in both °C and °F.

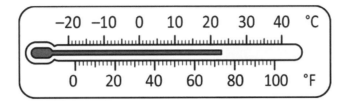

Write the temperature that the thermometer is showing in °C.

°C

1 mark

21 Five babies were weighed when they were born.

baby	weight (kg)
A	6.4
B	5.9
C	7.3
D	6.0
E	6.9

What is the mean weight of the babies in grams?

Show your method

2 marks

Mathematics
Paper 3: reasoning

Instructions

Before you start

Make sure you have a pen, pencil, rubber, ruler, angles measurer or protractor and a mirror.

You are **not** allowed to use a calculator or tracing paper.

Questions and answers

If you need to do working out, you can use the space around the question.

Some questions have a method box like this:

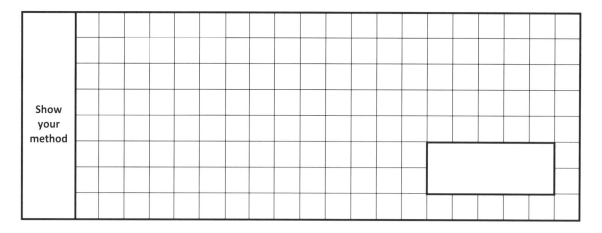

For these questions you may get a mark for showing your method.

Marks

The number at the side of the page tells you the maximum number of marks for each question.

1   The numbers in this sequence increase by 5 each time. The first term is –6

Write the first 8 terms of this sequence.

____   ____   ____   ____   ____   ____   ____   ____

1 mark

2   This is a table for sorting numbers.

Write one number in each box.

One is done for you.

	multiple of 6	not a multiple of 6
multiple of 9	18	
not a multiple of 9		

2 marks

3 Look at this number:

57,298.63

Write the digit that is in the thousands place.

1 mar

Write the digit that is in tenths place.

1 mar

4 A clock shows this time twice a day.

Tick the two 24-hour times that this time could be.

04:35   05:35   07:35   17:35   16:35

1 mark

5 Work out the values of *a* and *b* in the equations below.

5*a* = 85
3*a* + 4*b* = 95

a = _____   *b* = _____

2 marks

6 Write these numbers in order, starting with the largest.

5.9   4.007   0.56   0.709   4.009

largest   smallest

_____   _____   _____   _____   _____

1 mark

7 Use your knowledge of place value to complete each calculation.

9.2 × [ ] = 920

9.2 × [ ] = 92

9.2 ÷ [ ] = 0.0092

2 mark

8 Write the number 184,046 in words.

_____

1 mark

9 Sanjit has a piece of rope that is 6 metres long.
He cuts it into three pieces.
The length of the first piece is 2.67 metres.
The length of the second piece is 1.96 metres.

Work out the length of the third piece.
Give your answer in centimetres.

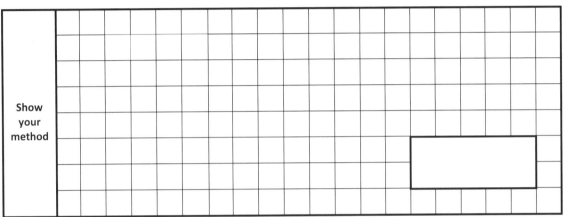

Show your method

2 marks

10 Look at the angle line below. Draw another line to form an obtuse angle.

1 mark

Measure your angle. Write its size on your drawing.

1 mark

11   Owen uses 64 small cubes to make a larger cube.

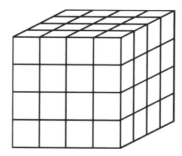

Write the letter of the cuboid that has the same volume as Owen's cube.

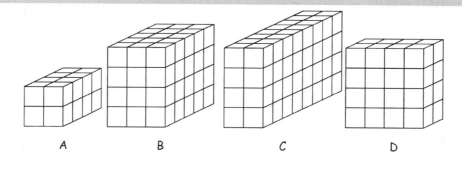

A   B   C   D

_____

1 mark

12   A school orders 12 boxes of exercise books.
Each box contains 3 packs of exercise books.
Each pack contains 32 exercise books.

How many exercise books does the school order in total?

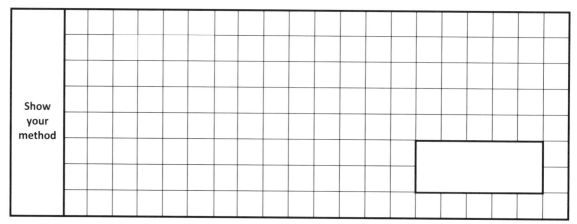

Show your method

2 marks

13 Jill chooses a number less than 50. She divides it by 3 and then adds 9
She then divides this result by 5. Her answer is 4.8

What was the number she started with?

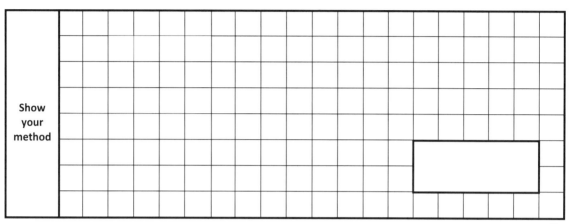

Show your method

2 marks

14 Complete this table by rounding the numbers to the nearest thousand.

	rounded to the nearest thousand
545,890	
54,589	
5,458.9	

2 marks

15 Write the four missing digits to make this addition correct.

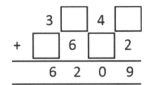

2 mark

16 A bag contains black and white counters.

Write the ratio of white to black counters.

Give your answer in its simplest form.

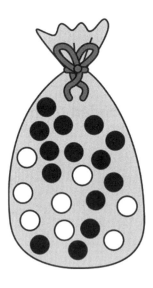

1 mar

17 George found that 8 toy soldiers have the same weight as 3 toy horses.

The weight of one toy soldier is 135 g.

What is the weight of one toy horse?

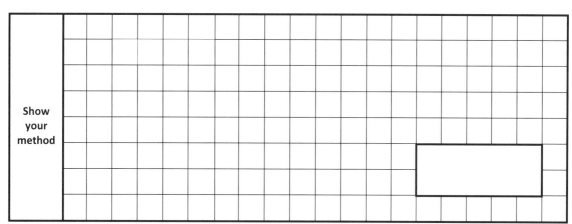

Show your method

2 marks

18 The base of a parallelogram is 23 cm. Its perpendicular height is 12 cm.

What is the area of the parallelogram?

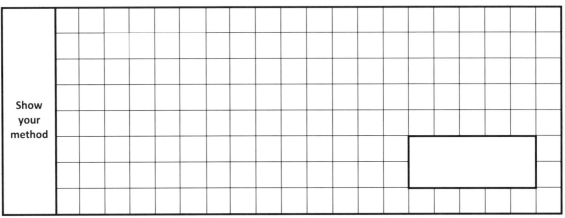

Show your method

2 mark

19 A school spent £156.80 on PE mats.
It spent another £98.20 on other PE equipment.

It has $\frac{1}{4}$ of its PE budget left.

How much money was in the PE budget at the start?

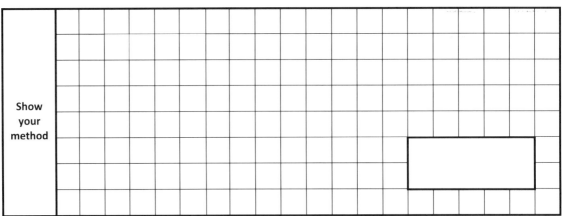

Show your method

2 mark

20

$23 \times 68 = 1,564$

Explain how you can use this fact to find the answer to 24×68

1 mark

21

A bag of 5 potatoes costs £3.00
A bag of 4 onions costs £2.60

How much more does one onion cost than one potato?

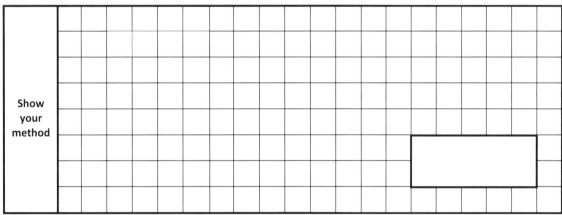

Show your method

2 marks

ARITHMETIC CHALLENGE: ANSWERS

1. 1,007

2. 308

3. 43.5

4. 567

5. 1,122

6. 16

7. 42,515

8. 705

9. 60

10. 1,929

11. 637

12. 5,600

13. 318,000

14. 7,245

15. 126

16. 48.187

17. 78.19

18. 128,766

19. 116

20. 0.006

21. 6.75

22. 115

23. 4,134 (2 marks: 1 mark for correct method; full marks for correct answer, irrespective of method)

24. $\frac{13}{8}$ or $1\frac{5}{8}$

25. 240

26. 87.6

27. $\frac{7}{10}$

28. 26 (2 marks: 1 mark for correct method; full marks for correct answer, irrespective of method)

29. 66

30. 219,297 (2 marks: 1 mark for correct method; full marks for correct answer, irrespective of method)

31. $\frac{23}{8}$ or $2\frac{7}{8}$

32. 48,598 (2 marks: 1 mark for correct method; full marks for correct answer, irrespective of method)

33. $\frac{1}{5}$

34. 99

35. $\frac{19}{12}$ or $1\frac{7}{12}$

36. 4

Total: 40 marks

UMBER, RATIO AND ALGEBRA CHALLENGE: ANSWERS

290, 370 (1 mark)

60 (1 mark)

■ = 19; O = 23 (2 marks)

3 : 1 (1 mark)

a) 120   212   298   305
b) 398   298
c) 120 (3 marks)

a) $f + 9 = 25$ b) 16 (2 marks)

1 : 5 (1 mark)

£1,987 £2,009 £3,809 £3,899 £6,845
(1 mark)

16 are left in the jar (2 marks: 1 mark for method, 1 mark for correct answer)

0. $m = 15$ (1 mark)

1. 13 boys, 39 girls (2 marks)

2. $s = 30$ (1 mark)

13. a) $t = 0.95m + 0.50$, where m is the number of litres and t is the total price in pounds
b) £5.25 (2 marks)

14. 38, 31, 24, 17, 10, 3, −4, −11 (1 mark)

15. 778 − 297 = 481 (2 marks: 1 mark for two correct numbers; full marks for three correct numbers)

16. 48 men and 12 women (2 marks)

17. a) 2001   b) MMX (2 marks)

18. 3.05 (1 mark)

19. a) £30   b) £42 (2 marks)

20. a) 280,000   b) 278,000
c) 278,470 (3 marks)

21. a) 60 cakes   b) 25 g
c) 10 eggs (3 marks)

22. a) 5,999,989 b) 7,990,000 (2 marks)

23. 19, 57, 38 (2 marks: 1 mark for correct method; full marks for correct answer, irrespective of method)

Total: 40 marks

GEOMETRY, MEASUREMENT AND STATISTICS CHALLENGE: ANSWERS

1. A = circle, B = pentagon, C = octagon, D = sphere, E = cylinder, F = hexagonal prism (3 marks: 1 mark for 2 correct answers; 2 marks for 4 correct answers; 3 marks for 6 correct answers)

2. 0.45 m   67 cm   100 cm   1.45 m   156 cm   (1 mark)

3.

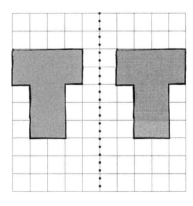

(1 mark)

4. obtuse (1 mark)

5.

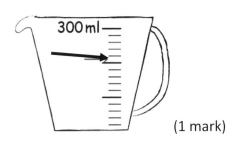

(1 mark)

6. a) £98,050   b) £463,645 (2 marks)

7. 643 ml (1 mark)

8. 37° (1 mark)

9.

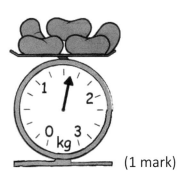

(1 mark)

10. a) clock should show 3:30 (hour hand half way between 3 and 4, minute hand at 6)
     b) 15:30 (2 marks)

OMETRY, MEASUREMENT AND STATISTICS CHALLENGE: ANSWERS

. a) 13:25   b) 25 minutes   c) 52 minutes (3 marks)

. 442.5 g (2 marks: 1 mark for method, 1 for correct answer)

. Any shape with an area of 6 squares and a perimeter of 14 squares. (1 mark)

. 4, 2 (1 mark)

. 34 mm   b) 110° (2 marks) Note that these answers may differ depending on printer settings.

. a) June   b) £35   c) £60 (3 marks)

. a)

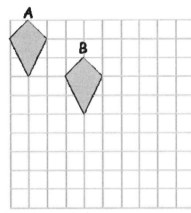

b) 3, 2 (2 marks)

8. 35p (2 marks: 1 mark for method, 1 mark for correct answer)

9. a) one set of parallel lines marked   b) two sets of parallel lines marked
c) two sets of parallel lines marked   d) no sets of parallel lines   e) no sets of parallel lines
(2 marks: 1 mark for 3 correct answers, full marks for all correct)

0. 546 square metres (2 marks: 1 mark for method, 1 mark for correct answer)

1. (−3, 3)   (3, 3)   (5, −3)   (−5, −3) (2 marks: 1 mark for 2 correct coordinates; 2 marks for 4
correct coordinates)

2. 27 (1 mark)

3. Check student's plotting is correct and titles are accurate for what the graph is showing. (2 marks: 1
for correct plotting of points; 1 for appropriate title and labels)

Total: 40 marks

TOPIC TESTS: ANSWERS

1 DIAGNOSTIC

1. a) triangle b) parallelogram c) trapezium d) cylinder
   e) sphere f) tetrahedron (6 marks)
2. square-based pyramid (1 mark)
3. $m = 6$ (1 mark)
4. 0.8 and 80% (2 marks)

2 PLACE VALUE

1. 888, 898, 989, 998, 1,005, 1,045 (1 mark)
2. Any number from 500,001 to 999,999 (1 mark)
3. 2.078 2.909 2.990 3.001 3.678 (1 mark)
4. a) 9 b) 3,098,045 c) 3,091,145 d) 902,855
   (5 marks: a – c = 1 mark each; d = 1 mark for method, 1 mark for correct answer)
5. 98.367 (2 marks)

3 ROUNDING

1. a) 6,083,460 b) 6,083,500 c) 6,083,000 d) 6,080,000
   e) 6,100,000 (5 marks)
2. a) 17 b) 179 c) 24.9 d) 99.9
   e) 14.0 (5 marks)

4 ESTIMATING

1. a) 3000 + 1000 = 4000 b) 500 – 200 = 300 (2 marks)
2. a) 320 + 90 = 410 b) 190 + 30 + 60 = 280 c) 320 + 190 = 510
   d) 320 + 90 + 60 + 30 + 190 + 30 = 720 (8 marks: 1 mark for method, 1 mark for correct answer per part)

5 ADDITION

1. a) 16,889 b) 997,121 (2 marks)
2. a) 160,293 b) 211,745 (3 marks: a = 1 mark; b = 1 mark for method, 1 mark for correct answer)
3. a) 37,665 b) 29.830 c) 55,730 (5 marks: a = 1 mark; b – c = 1 mark for method, 1 mark for correct answer each)

⊃PIC TESTS: ANSWERS

ЅUBTRACTION

a) 3,567   b) 21,432   c) 111,031   d) 333,021 (4 marks)

a) 188,892   b) 908,710 (2 marks)

a) 10,198   b) 10,837 (3 marks: a = 1 mark; b = 1 mark for method,
1 mark for correct answer)

772 km (1 mark)

MULTIPLES AND FACTORS

any from: a) 1, 3, 6, 11, 22, 33, 66   b) 1, 2, 4, 5, 8, 10, 16, 20, 40, 80

c) 1, 2, 3, 4, 6, 8, 9, 12, 18, 24, 36, 72 (6 marks: for each part, 1 mark for 2 correct answers; 2 marks
for 3 correct anwers)

2, 3, 5, 7, 11, 13, 17, 19, 23, 29 (1 mark per 5 correctly identified)

multiples of 10: 70   multiples of 8: 32, 56   common multiples of 8 and 10: 40, 80
multiples of neither 8 nor 10: 17, 92 (2 marks: 1 mark for identifying multiples of 10 and 8; 1 mark for
identifying common and non-multiples)

SQUARES AND CUBES

. It is the answer to 7 × 7 and square numbers are the product of numbers multiplied
  by themselves. (1 mark)

. It is the answer to 6 × 6 × 6 and cube numbers are the product of numbers multiplied by themselves
  twice. (1 mark)

. a) 36 + 81 = 117   b) 125 + 216 = 341   c) 343 − 16 = 327   d) 729 − 64 = 665
(8 marks: 2 marks per part 1 mark for correct method; full marks for correct answer, irrespective
of method)

MULTIPLICATION

.. a) 34,500   b) 509,000   c) 986,700   d) 1,308,000 (4 marks)

ℤ. a) 76,032   b) 23,884 (2 marks)

ᴫ. a) 5,110   b) 21,632 (4 marks: 1 mark for method, 1 mark for correct answer per part)

‍0 DIVISION

ᴫ. a) 9   b) 7 (2 marks)

ℤ. a) 245.5   b) 342 (2 marks)

ℬ. a) 253 r 12   b) 213 (4 marks: 1 mark for method, 1 mark for correct answer per part)

ᴫ. 147 bags (2 marks: 1 mark for method, 1 mark for correct answer)

TOPIC TESTS: ANSWERS

11 ORDER OF OPERATIONS

1. a) 88   b) 423   c) 104   d) 69 (4 marks)

2. $(6 \times 12) + 38 = 110$ (2 marks: 1 mark for method and 1 mark for correct answer)

3. $(9 \times 16) - 25 = 119$ (2 marks: 1 mark for method and 1 mark for correct answer)

4. $(63 + 27) \div 9 = 10$ (2 marks: 1 mark for method and 1 mark for correct answer)

12 PROPER FRACTIONS

1. a) $\frac{4}{9}$ and any equivalent fraction   b) $\frac{8}{12}$ and any equivalent fraction

c) $\frac{3}{15}$ and any equivalent fraction (6 marks: 2 per part for 2 correct answers)

2. a) $\frac{1}{3}$ b) $\frac{1}{4}$ c) $\frac{6}{11}$ d) $\frac{2}{15}$ (4 marks)

13 FRACTIONS GREATER THAN 1

1. a) $\frac{11}{3}$ b) $\frac{11}{2}$ c) $\frac{48}{5}$ (3 marks)

2. a) $5\frac{5}{6}$ b) $6\frac{2}{7}$ c) $5\frac{6}{9}$ or $5\frac{2}{3}$ (3 marks)

3. a) $\frac{5}{7} > \frac{4}{35}$ b) $\frac{7}{8} < \frac{58}{64}$ c) $1\frac{4}{9} < \frac{40}{27}$ d) $\frac{70}{60} < 2\frac{7}{12}$ (4 marks)

14 ADDING AND SUBTRACTING FRACTIONS

1. a) for example: $\frac{14}{22}$, $\frac{21}{33}$, $\frac{70}{110}$, $\frac{700}{1100}$

b) for example: $\frac{4}{5}$, $\frac{16}{20}$, $\frac{24}{30}$, $\frac{80}{100}$ (4 marks: 1 mark per 2 correct answers)

2. a) $1\frac{1}{2}$ b) 2   c) $2\frac{3}{7}$ (6 marks: 1 mark for method, 1 mark for correct answer per part)

15 MULTIPLYING FRACTIONS AND DECIMALS

1. a) 598   b) 50 (2 marks)

2. a) $4\frac{2}{7}$ b) $1\frac{5}{9}$ (2 marks)

3. a) 12.15   b) 14.8 (2 marks)

4. a) $\frac{32}{63}$ b) $\frac{33}{56}$ (4 marks: 1 mark for method, 1 mark for correct answer per part)

MATHS
— YEAR 6 —

OPIC TESTS: ANSWERS

DIVIDING FRACTIONS AND DECIMALS

a) 0.678   b) 0.0305   c) 0.01207 (3 marks)

a) $\frac{7}{104}$ b) $\frac{9}{98}$ c) $\frac{1}{18}$ (3 marks)

a) 0.25   b) 0.2 (4 marks: 1 mark for method, 1 mark for correct answer per part)

7 PERCENTAGES

a) 76%   b) 70% (2 marks)

a) 40%   b) 65%   c) 68%   d) 84% (4 marks)

16% (1 mark)

a) 55   b) 40.7 (3 marks: a = 1 mark; b = 1 mark for method, 1 mark for correct answer)

8 EQUIVALENCE

Percentage	Decimal	Fraction
20%	0.2	$\frac{1}{5}$
64%	0.64	$\frac{16}{25}$
36%	0.36	$\frac{9}{25}$

(6 marks)

a) 0.7   b) $\frac{1}{5}$ c) $\frac{1}{10}$ d) $\frac{13}{20}$ (4 marks)

19 RATIO

1. a) ratio 2 : 3, proportion striped $\frac{3}{5}$ b) ratio 13 : 11, proportion striped $\frac{11}{24}$

c) ratio 4 : 9, proportion striped $\frac{9}{13}$ (6 marks: 1 mark per correct answer)

2. £31.50 and £73.50 (2 marks)

3. 18 cars (2 marks: 1 mark for method, 1 mark for correct answer)

TOPIC TESTS: ANSWERS

20 SCALE FACTORS

1.

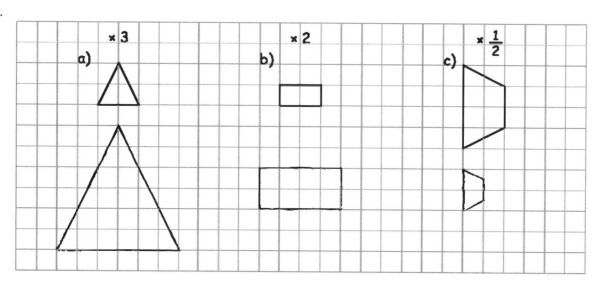

(3 marks

2. 9 (2 marks)
3. 4 (2 marks: 1 mark for method, 1 mark for correct answer)
4. 10 cm × 14 cm (3 marks: 2 marks for method, 1 mark for correct answer)

21 SIMPLE FORMULAE

1. a) 350   b) 12   c) 138 (3 marks)
2. a) 2.5   b) 6   c) 9 (3 marks)
3. a) 400   b) 65 (4 marks: 1 mark for method, 1 mark for correct answer each)

22 LINEAR SEQUENCES

1. a) 36   b) 49 (2 marks)
2. a) 59, 67   term-to-term rule: add 4
   b) 74, 58   term-to-term rule: subtract 8
   (6 marks: 1 mark per correct number in sequence, 1 mark for rule)
3. 17, 26, 35, 44, 53, 62 (2 marks: 1 mark for each 3 correct numbers in sequence)

ɔPIC TESTS: ANSWERS

TWO UNKNOWNS

a) $j = 19, k = 13$ $j = 18, k = 14$ $j = 17, k = 15$ $j = 16, k = 16$ $j = 15, k = 17$
   $j = 14, k = 18$ $j = 13, k = 19$

b) $m = 30, n = 26$ $m = 29, n = 27$ $m = 28, n = 28$ $m = 27, n = 29$ $m = 26, n = 30$

c) $d = 20, c = 5$ $d = 19, c = 4$ $d = 18, c = 3$ $d = 17, c = 2,$ $d = 16, c = 1$

(6 marks: award 1 mark for 3 correct answers in a part; award 2 marks for all correct answers in a part)

ɔak librarian	hazel librarian	rowan librarian	sycamore librarian	beech librarian
ɔak sports captain	hazel sports captain	rowan sports captain	sycamore sports captain	beech sports captain
ɔak register ɱonitor	hazel register monitor	rowan register monitor	sycamore register monitor	beech register monitor
ɔak snack monitor	hazel snack monitor	rowan snack monitor	sycamore snack monitor	beech snack monitor

× 5 = 20 combinations so 20 children are needed (4 marks: 3 marks for method, 1 mark for ɔrrect answer)

₄ SCALES AND UNITS

convert to ml	convert to m	convert to km	convert to kg
11.078 litres = **11,078 ml**	808 cm = **8.08 m**	307 m = **0.307 km**	1,056 g = **1.056 kg**
0.986 litres = **986 ml**	1,950 cm = **19.5 m**	11,067 m = **11.067 km**	10,011 g = **10.011 kg**

(4 marks: 1 mark for each 2 correct answers)

2. a) 10 inches   b) 6 pints   c) 360 grams (6 marks: 1 for method, 1 for correct answer per part)

25 WORKING WITH UNITS

1. a) £1.09   b) £0.84   c) £101.07   d) £2,011.00 (4 marks)

2. a) 67 cm   680 mm   1.56 m   67 m   0.8 km
   b) 12 g   110 g   208 g   1.09 kg   3.9 kg (4 marks: award 1 mark per part for 3 correct answers; award 2 marks per part for all correct answers)

3. 35.429 litres (2 marks: 1 mark for method, 1 mark for correct answer)

TOPIC TESTS: ANSWERS

26 TIME

1. a) 2010   b) 35 (2 marks)

2. a) clock hands showing 9:50 with pm written next to it

   b) clock hands showing 5:20 with am written next to it

   c) clock hands showing 1:15 with pm written next to it

   (6 marks: 1 mark for correct clock hands, 1 mark for correct am / pm)

3. 4:35 pm (2 marks: 1 mark for method, 1 mark for correct answer)

27 PERIMETER

1. a) 52 cm   b) 66 cm (2 marks)

2. a) 26 cm   b) 26 m   c) 28 cm

   (8 marks: 1 mark for method, 1 mark for correct answer per part)

28 AREA OF A RECTANGLE

1. a) 108   b) 600   c) 56   d) 20 (4 marks)

2. 231 cm^2 (2 marks: 1 mark for method, 1 for correct answer)

3. table 1 = 3.6 m^2 table 2 = 0.48 m^2 table 3 = 2.25 m^2 total = 6.33 m^2 (4 marks)

29 AREAS OF OTHER SHAPES

1. a) 58.5 cm^2 b) 16.25 cm^2 (4 marks: 1 mark for method, 1 mark for correct answer per part)

2. 315 cm^2 (2 marks: 1 mark for method, 1 mark for correct answer)

3. a) 96 cm^2 b) 372 cm^2 (4 marks: 1 mark for method, 1 mark for correct answer per part)

30 VOLUME

1. 84 cm^3 (2 marks: 1 mark for method, 1 mark for correct answer)

2. 585 cm^3 (2 marks: 1 mark for method, 1 mark for correct answer)

3. 4,158 cm^3 (2 marks: 1 mark for method, 1 mark for correct answer)

4. 13,500 cm^3 (2 marks: 1 mark for method, 1 mark for correct answer)

5. 42.875 m^3 (2 marks: 1 mark for method, 1 mark for correct answer)

31 2D SHAPES

1. a) heptagon, regular   b) quadrilateral (trapezium), regular   c) nonagon, regular

   d) pentagon, irregular   e) quadrilateral (rhombus or diamond), irregular

   (10 marks: 2 per part, 1 for regular/irregular, 1 for naming correct shape)

OPIC TESTS: ANSWERS

2 3D SHAPES

a) sphere   b) cylinder   c) square-based pyramid (3 marks)

shape	faces	vertices	edges
tetrahedron	4	4	6
hexagonal prism	8	12	18

(6 marks)

. pentagonal prism (1 mark)

3 ANGLES

. a) 40° (acute) b) 116° (obtuse) (4 marks)
. a) 72°   b) 64°   c) 50°   d) 75° (4 marks)
. a) 16 cm   b) 68 cm (2 marks)

4 TRANSFORMATIONS

. A = (6, 5)   B = (−4, 7)   C = (−6, −10)   D = (8, −3) (1 mark for all correct)

.. a)
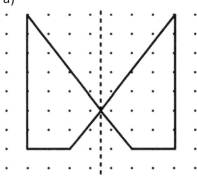

b)
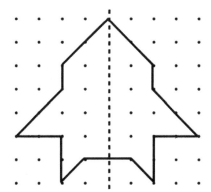

(6 marks)

3. A = (6, 8)   B = (10, 10)   C = (10, 4) (3 marks: 1 mark per correct answer)

TOPIC TESTS: ANSWERS

35 TABLES

1.

favourite flavour	number of children	percentage of children
strawberry	40	20%
vanilla	50	25%
chocolate	60	30%
mint	30	15%
other	20	10%

(6 marks)

2. a) 1 hour and 10 minutes b) 38 minutes c) 30 minutes d) 11.40 am (4 marks)

36 CHARTS

1. a) number of children b) colours c) 40 d) approximately 204
(5 marks: a–c = 1 mark each; d = 1 mark for method, 1 mark for correct answer)
2. a) 25% b) 'walk' sector circled c) 25% d) 50% e) about 35% (5 marks)

37 LINE GRAPHS

1. a) 12 °C b) 12:00, 18 °C c) 00:00, 10 °C
d) 8 °C e) 4 °C f) 3 °C
(10 marks: a and d = 1 mark per correct answer; b, c, e, f = 1 mark for method, 1 mark for correct answer)

38 MEAN AVERAGES

1. a) 14.2 cm c) 43p e) 1,004.4
b) 165.25 ml d) 83.8 f) £1.47
(7 marks: a–e = 1 mark per correct answer; f = 1 mark for method, 1 mark for correct answer)
2. 15 (3 marks: 2 marks for method, 1 mark for correct answer)

PRACTICE PAPER: ANSWERS

PAPER 1: ARITHMETIC

1,003

486

5.8

96

1,765

6

867

5.64

162

0. $\frac{4}{7}$

1. 80

2. 456

3. 49

4. 74,500

5. 100,000

6. 150

7. 960

8. 11.12

9. $\frac{8}{11}$

20. 11,865

21. 1,459

22. 6.955

23. 1,638 (2 marks: 1 mark for method, 1 for correct answer)

24. 9.61

25. 267 (2 marks: 1 mark for method, 1 for correct answer)

26. $\frac{1}{27}$

27. 323

28. 421,961

29. 54,612 (2 marks: 1 mark for method, 1 for correct answer)

30. 60

31. 4

32. 0.375 or $\frac{3}{8}$

33. 1.2 or $1\frac{1}{5}$ or $\frac{6}{5}$

34. 59 (2 marks: 1 mark for method, 1 for correct answer)

35. $\frac{22}{144} = \frac{11}{72}$ (2 marks: 1 mark for method, 1 for correct answer)

36. 0.3125 or $\frac{5}{16}$

Total: 40 marks

PRACTICE PAPER: ANSWERS

PAPER 2: REASONING

1. 678   815 (2 marks)

2. 120 or 150 or 180   250   350 (2 marks)

3. 198 + 426 = 624 (2 marks)

4. Oslo   18 °C (2 marks)

5. prime numbers = 7, 19, 71, 89
   prime and even = 2
   even numbers = 14, 46
   even and cube = 8, 64
   cube numbers = 27, 125 (2 marks)

6. 4 : 5   1 : 1 (2 marks)

7. £78,500   £99,705   £101,867
   £101,890   £110,689   (1 mark)

8. 0.2 and 0.25 (1 mark)

9. 75p (2 marks: 1 mark for method, 1 mark for
   correct answer)

10. 3 triangles shaded
   6 rectangles shaded
   12 squares shaded (2 marks)

11. 5 hours and 46 minutes (1 mark)

12. 14:58 (1 mark)

13. C = £0.76n + £1.20   £8.80   16
   (1 mark for first two parts, 2 marks for third
   part showing method and correct answer)

14. 45 days (2 marks: 1 for method, 1 for
   correct answer)

15. 3 (1 mark)

16. 21, 42, 63 (1 mark)

17. 4 (1 mark)

18. 62 × 35 (2 marks)

19. P = (−10, −40)   Q = (10, −40)
   R = (−20, 30)   (1 mark)

20. 23°C (1 mark)

21. 6500 g (2 marks: 1 for method, 1 for
   correct answer)

Total: 35 mar

PRACTICE PAPER: ANSWERS

PAPER 3: REASONING

−6, −1, 4, 9, 14, 19, 24, 29 (1 mark)

	multiple of 6	not a multiple of 6
multiple of 9	18	e.g. 9, 27, 45…
not a multiple of 9	e.g. 6, 12, 24, 30…	e.g. 5, 7, 8, 10…

(2 marks)

7   6 (2 marks)

05:35 and 17:35 (1 mark)

a = 17   *b* = 11 (2 marks)

5.9   4.009   4.007   0.709   0.56 (1 mark)

100   10   1,000 (2 marks)

one hundred and eighty-four thousand and forty-six. (1 mark)

137 centimetres (2 marks: 1 mark for method, 1 mark for correct answer)

10. Check student's drawing and measurement of angle. (2 marks)

11. C (1 mark)

12. 1,152 exercise books (2 marks: 1 mark for method, 1 mark for correct answer)

13. 45 (2 marks: 1 mark for method, 1 mark for correct answer)

14.

	rounded to the nearest thousand
545,890	546,000
54,589	55,000
5,458.9	5,000

(2 marks)

15. 3547 + 2662 = 6209 (2 marks)

16. 4 : 7 (1 mark)

17. 360 g (2 marks: 1 mark for method, 1 mark for correct answer)

PRACTICE PAPER: ANSWERS

PAPER 3: REASONING

18. 276 cm^2 (2 marks: 1 mark for method, 1 mark for correct answer)

19. £340 (2 marks: 1 mark for method, 1 mark for correct answer)

20. The answer will be 68 more than the answer in the multiplication given, e.g. 1,632 (1 mark)

21. 5 pence (2 marks: 1 mark for method, 1 mark for correct answer)

Total: 35 mar

olished by Pearson Education Limited, 80 Strand, London, WC2R 0RL.

vw.pearsonschools.co.uk

xt © Pearson Education Limited 2016
ries consultant: Margaret Reeve
ited by Elektra Media Ltd
esigned by Andrew Magee
peset by Elektra Media Ltd
oduced by Elektra Media Ltd
iginal illustrations © Pearson Education Limited 2016
ustrated by Elektra Media Ltd
over design by Andrew Magee

e right of Rachel Axten-Higgs to be identified as author of this work has been asserted by her in accordance with the
opyright, Designs and Patents Act 1988.

rst published 2016

) 18 17 16
) 9 8 7 6 5 4 3 2 1

ritish Library Cataloguing in Publication Data
catalogue record for this book is available from the British Library

BN 978 1 292 17252 1

rinted in the United Kingdom by Ashford Colour Press Ltd

Acknowledgements

We would like to thank Tutora for its invaluable help in the development and trialling of this course.